Merry Christmas, 1965
from
Rita

Reread entire book 5/8/83

BEYOND THE COMMANDMENTS

BEYOND THE COMMANDMENTS

JAMES KILLGALLON
GERARD WEBER

HERDER AND HERDER

1964
HERDER AND HERDER NEW YORK
232 Madison Avenue, New York 16, N.Y.

First edition 1964
Second impression 1965

Nihil obstat: Edward J. Sutfin
Censor Librorum

Imprimatur: Patrick C. Brennan
Vicar General, Diocese of Burlington
December 3, 1963

The *nihil obstat* and *imprimatur* are official declarations that a book or pamphlet is free of doctrinal or moral error. No implication is contained therein that those who have granted the *nihil obstat* and *imprimatur* agree with the contents, opinions or statements expressed.

Library of Congress Catalog Card Number: 64-13687

Printed in the United States of America

CONTENTS

INTRODUCTION

THE MATURE CHRISTIAN

Every now and then a potential sponsor for Baptism or Confirmation comes to the rectory seeking a letter testifying to the fact that he or she is a "practical Catholic." Often enough, the priest who is expected to write the letter has never, to his knowledge, set eyes on the person. A check of the parish files may or may not show that he is registered in the parish. The fact of registration, in any event, proves only that the person wishes to be identified with the parish; it doesn't tell, really, what kind of Catholic he is. What usually happens is that the priest asks, "Do you go to Mass on Sundays and make your Easter duty?" These seem to be the requirements which qualify one as a "practical Catholic" as the term is generally used. But the term itself is surely not very clear. Is a "practical Catholic" the same as a "good Catholic"? And what, for that matter, is a "good Catholic"?

John and Mary Smith go to Mass every Sunday. They are honest; they do not practice birth control; they send their children to the Catholic school. They also think that Negroes "should be kept in their place," and that the popes have no business writing about all this "social stuff" in their encyclicals. Are the Smiths "good Catholics"? José Gonzales, on the other hand, who came from a little town in Puerto Rico, does not go to Mass on Sunday and sends his children to the public school. He never did get around to having his marriage "blessed" by a priest, because he never managed to save up enough money to give what he considers the necessary offering to the Church and to provide the party which his friends would expect. José has a deep sense of responsibility toward his neighbors. He has been known to take a whole family into his apartment to live when both the father and the mother were out of work. He thinks that being a Christian means, first of all, treating all men as your brothers and sharing what you have with them. If José came in for a letter stating that he was a good or practical Catholic he could hardly expect to get it. But how about the Smiths? Would it be out of order for the priest not only to ask about Mass and the sacraments but also to inquire, "And what are your views on segregation?" and "Do you accept the teachings of the popes as found in the encyclicals?"

Frequently the norm used in determining who is a good Catholic is canon law and the ten commandments, understood in a narrow and negative sense, as if ours were a religion merely of duties. Those who live up to their duties are considered to be good Catholics. The Church is Christ, and we cannot conceive of Christ saying that we do not have to live up to our duties and keep the commandments. Nevertheless, the norm which Christ gave was a much more positive and far-reaching one: "By this will all men know that you are my disciples, if you have love for one another" (Jn 13:35).

May we say, therefore, that a good Catholic is a Catholic who loves his neighbor and also lives up to his duties as a Catholic? But would not a good Catholic also be expected to be one who has the same mind as the Church, who knows the Church's teachings and sees their application to his life, who knows the Church's teaching in relation to the great issues and problems of the modern world, one whose prayer life is truly Catholic, one who enters wholeheartedly into the liturgy? In short, is not the term "good Catholic" too vague? Apart from the letters which sponsors for Baptism need, in which case the phrase has a narrow meaning, would it not be better to use a different term, one which can be defined more precisely? If we are speaking of what Catholics ought to be or ought to be striving to become, we might better speak of spiritual maturity. This is what the Church tries to help her members attain. The question, then, might well be, what is a mature Catholic, or what is religious maturity?

A person's growth toward maturity is a phenomenon of everyday life. We are all amused at the young boy who peers eagerly into the mirror, studying the fuzz on his upper lip, looking forward to the day when it will be real hair and he will be able to shave. The same boy takes great delight in showing off his muscles, especially if a female in his age bracket is present. The boy is growing up. His body is developing. He is becoming aware of his strength. He is impatiently awaiting the time when he will be in full possession of his powers. Those about him sometimes share his impatience. When he gets in a temper or sulks because he can't have his way, his parents ask themselves, "When will he grow up?" If he lies around the house during the summer, he will be told to grow up and go out and get a job. There will be discussions from time to time about how grown up the teen-ager is. Is he grown up enough, for example, to drive the car? All this is part of the maturing process. We have all experienced it; we all live with it. It is so much a part of our lives that we often fail to stop and analyze what it means to be grown up, to be mature.

Physical maturity is not difficult to see and define. There comes a time when all living things reach the peak of their physical development. The story is told of an Oriental potentate who left orders that he was to be awakened in the middle of the night in order to enjoy his favorite type of melon at the moment it reached perfect ripeness. Things mature at different rates: the century plant takes a long time to reach its maturity; a tiny shoot takes years to develop into a beautiful, spreading shade tree. The gangling boy who was so clumsy he used to trip over his own feet begins to move gracefully down the basketball floor and to shoot in the low eighties on the golf course. The little girl with stringy hair who used to romp in the lot with the boys becomes the Miss America of the block, the recipient of appreciative whistles as she walks sedately down the street.

A man reaches his physical maturity in his early twenties, but he still has a lot of growing up to do. Intellectual maturity comes more slowly. A man's most creative years may be his late twenties and early thirties, but his mind keeps developing as long as he is interested in learning. Social maturity usually comes in the middle thirties, when a man finds his place in society and is fully at ease with other people and confident of himself. Real emotional maturity may not come until the forties. A man must do a lot of living and thinking before he reaches the stage at which he really knows himself and accepts himself for what he is.

It is more difficult to describe psychic maturity. It is easier to describe its opposite. The wife who is a clinging vine and depends on her husband for every decision is not mature; she is still a little girl. The man who explodes in anger when someone crosses him is not mature; he is still a little boy. Undoubtedly, one of the signs of maturity is the ability to make up one's mind, to lay and follow a course of one's own choosing. The person who remains calm in a time of crisis is giving evidence of maturity: he is sure of himself and his resources, and is not easily threatened by outside forces.

Such maturity was shown by a famous secretary of state, paradoxically enough, when he lost his temper at a high-level meeting. Noted for his icy calmness, he sat listening to an attack on himself and his policies. As he listened and mentally prepared his defense, he began to wonder idly whether it would be even possible for him to become really angry; it had been so many years since he had lost his temper that he could not remember how it felt. The more he thought about it the more interesting the idea became. He actually made an effort to become angry. Within a few minutes he was on his feet, shouting and ready to fight. Loss of temper in this man was actually a sign of his maturity; it pointed up his marvelous habitual self-control. Only he could provoke himself to anger; nothing outside of him could do so.

Emotional, social, and intellectual maturity demand

two things. One is an honest evaluation of one's talents and abilities; the other is the setting of good and attainable goals. The mature man has a true picture of himself. He sees himself as he really is—not so good as his mother thinks he is, not so bad as his enemies paint him. The immature person has not appraised his powers and abilities correctly. The Little Leaguer is sure that one day he will be playing for the Yankees; the little girl in dancing class dreams of becoming a great ballerina, though her teacher knows that she simply does not have the grace and coordination to become even a member of a ballet company. As a person matures he sees himself more realistically. The youth who wanted to be a drummer in a band recognizes the fact that he doesn't have a keen sense of rhythm but that he does have ability as a teacher. The boy who hated art in school discovers that he can make beautiful things with his hands and begins to develop the talent.

Everyone has some natural talent, but it often takes years for him to appreciate what he has. A young man who was shy with people had a difficult time keeping a job. He found a job as an accountant, but lost it. Discouraged, he took an aptitude test. It showed that he was not at all suited to work with figures but that, surprisingly enough, he had ability as a salesman. He found a job as a salesman and, using his newly discovered ability to deal with people, overcame his shyness and did well at his job. He had grown up; he had achieved confidence in himself and with his life. Men who strive to do things for which they are not suited are unhappy and frustrated. Men who are not using the talents they have are also unhappy and frustrated. The mature man adjusts his goals to meet changing conditions as he goes through life. His physical and mental powers undergo changes; his financial and social positions change. The mature man takes all these things into consideration. What once seemed to be out of the question may now be possible of achievement, and conversely what was a burning ambition back in high-school or college days may now be recognized as impractical and quietly put aside.

Religious maturity, like any other kind of maturity, is achieved only after a process of growth. It, too, is involved with goals which are attainable, with knowledge of self and one's potential, and with the development of one's powers toward the attainment of goals. The goals a person sets for himself in his growth toward religious maturity must be in line with his potential; goals he set for himself as a child must give way to other goals as changes occur. Most of the little boys and girls in second or third grade in any parochial school will raise their hands in response to the question, "How many of you are going to be priests or sisters when you grow up?" It will be a different story when they reach the eighth grade; the changes which take place with the onset of adolescence will have brought about a change in goals.

Acquiring convictions is an important part of the process of religious maturation. A child needs the guidance of his parents in order to do what is necessary for his own good. He obeys because he is told to. As he grows up he becomes free from parental control. He knows the reasons for the laws and rules and regulations. He does what he ought to do now on conviction, with an understanding of why he is to act. The Christian who is obsessed with the idea of keeping the laws of God and the Church simply because they are laws is religiously immature. The Christian who does not develop freedom and does not come to a deeper understanding of his faith is likewise religiously immature. The mature man has a better picture of himself when he is thiry-five than he had when he was nine or fifteen; the Catholic man who at thirty-five still makes his confession as he did when he was nine or fifteen is religiously immature. He has not grown in knowledge of himself, and he has not come to a deeper appreciation of the sacrament of Penance. The Christian who does not pray better as he grows older, who does not have a better understanding of the Mass, who does not participate in the Mass is religiously immature. The Catholic who is content to be a "practical Catholic" in the sense in which the term was used above is religiously immature.

Many Catholics would say that their goal in life is the salvation of their soul. A person with only this goal in mind will never reach religious maturity. The goal is not high enough; it is not the one set by our Lord. "You are to be perfect even as your heavenly Father is perfect," Jesus said. St. Paul, echoing these words, wrote to all Christians in his letter to the Thessalonians, "This is the will of God, your sanctification." And this sanctification is not to be worked out in a vacuum. St. Paul makes the context in which each member of the Mystical Body is to attain sanctification very concrete: as a member of that Body, in union with the other members of that Body, as a member of the Church, doing the work of the Church, the work of bringing all things to Christ and Christ to all things. The goal of God Himself in His plan of salvation for the world is the goal which each Christian must work for in becoming perfect as his heavenly Father. And that goal is, as St. Paul puts it, "to re-establish all things in Christ, both those in the heavens and those on the earth" (Eph 1:10).

The goal of the Christian, therefore, is not simply to save his own soul—to get to Heaven, as it were, all by himself and maybe by the skin of his teeth. It is to develop fully all the powers, natural and supernatural, with which God has endowed him by entering fully into the whole life and work of the Church. It is to attain the mind and heart of Christ as one lives the life of Christ and shares in the mission of Christ, the redemption and sanctification of the world, the completion and perfection of His Kingdom.

Christ and St. Paul state the goal of the Christian. They also show the means by which Christians are to attain that goal, and Christ gives that means: the Holy Spirit, the Spirit of Truth, Who teaches all truth, Who sanctifies and guides the members of Christ's Body and forms them in the image of Christ.

When a Christian takes stock of himself, appraising his powers in relation to the goal which God has set for him, he must do far more than assess his natural endowments. Indeed, these are meant to be used and must be examined realistically. It would be childish in the extreme to set out to become another Augustine or Thomas Aquinas if one's natural intellectual gifts were ordinary. But the Christian must also take into consideration the supernatural powers and aids which God gives him for the attainment of religious maturity. These powers will not normally enable a man to achieve miraculous results. Grace builds on nature; it transforms it, but it does not replace it or do violence to in. Yet God has set the goal of perfection for each of His children, to be attained in as many ways, perhaps, as there are children of God, and He gives all the supernatural help each will need to come to full Christian maturity.

First and foremost there is the Holy Spirit, the Spirit of Jesus, dwelling and acting within. There is God's all-important grace, without which we can do nothing toward the attainment of the goal. There are the Church, the Mass, the sacraments, and the aid of all in the Communion of Saints—our Lady, the saints in Heaven, and fellow members of the Mystical Body on earth. Neglect of these tremendous realities accounts for much stunted spiritual growth. One thing is certain: failure to grow and to attain religious maturity is never due to a lack of anything on God's part.

"You are to be perfect even as your heavenly Father is perfect" sounds at first like an impossible goal, and if it were taken literally it would be, of course. What Christ is actually saying in these words is that we are to strive to do the will of God perfectly, to make God's will our will in everything—in other words, to be like Him, Jesus Christ. It is no abstract model Christ is holding up to us; it is Himself.

The goal, then, is so to speak embodied in a person, Jesus Christ. The chief means to that goal is embodied in another person, the Spirit of Jesus, the Holy Spirit. It is the Spirit, as St. Paul points out, Who guides the Christian, not the Law which guided the Jews in the Old Testament. Christ sends this person into the Christian at Baptism and Confirmation. The Law, the guidance of the Spirit, and the meaning of the ten commandments in the life of a Christian will be treated in future chapters.

When St. Paul says that the Christian is not under the

Law he means two things. First of all, the Christian is not bound to observe the Law of the Torah, the multitudinous prescriptions of the Mosaic Law. Second, even the ten commandments have a different meaning for the Christian. He must observe them, of course, but they are no longer the norm; they are no longer the yardstick of his love of God. Now it is Christ Who unites men to God, not the Law. The Christian is baptized into Christ and thus lives with a new life, the life of Christ. His reason for not stealing should not be because there is a commandment which says, "Thou shalt not steal," but because Christ, in Whom he lives, is all holy, and stealing would be unthinkable in one who has put on Christ and been baptized into His Body. So it is with all the ten commandments. It is not that the Christian is free to disregard them, to break them, but rather that the Christian's goal is a much higher one than the observance of the ten commandments. His goal is to become Christlike. He is to follow the guidance not merely of the Law but of the Holy Spirit Whom Christ has sent into him. The mature Christian is not concerned, therefore, with keeping laws. He does what the Holy Spirit tells him to, speaking in his heart and through the Church, because he wants to do it. Therefore, he has the freedom of the Spirit.

If one were to ask a happy housewife what law she is obeying in doing the dishes and waxing the linoleum and making the beds, she would not know what the questioner was talking about. If she were to formulate an answer she would say, "It is not a question of law at all; I'm doing these things for my husband and children." Father Barnabas Mary Ahern, C.P., makes this point clear in an amusing example of a woman in prison who has to scrub floors and work in the prison laundry. She does these things grudgingly and only because she is compelled to do them. On no account will she do anything extra or find any joy or satisfaction in her work. She does it merely because she is bound by law to do it. But one fine day the woman falls in love with the warden. She is released from prison, and now lives in a house on the prison grounds as the wife of the warden. She performs the same tasks as before, but with what a different spirit! She does far more than her mere duties as a housewife would compel her to do. She is free and happy now in what she does. Such is the freedom of the Spirit which the mature Christian enjoys.

It is this freedom which Jesus Christ came to bring to all who would accept Him and become members of His Kingdom. It is the freedom to be really and fully oneself, a freedom which can only be enjoyed by one who has achieved religious maturity.

1

THE CHRISTIAN AND THE RULES

Charlie Williams approached the pearly gates with confidence. He should be well known in Heaven, he figured. After all, hadn't he been a Catholic all his life? Not a convert, not one of those who come into the Church when half their life is over, but a bona fide "born" Catholic. Meat had never passed his lips on a Friday. Charlie was sure that the celestial books contained an impressive report on all the salmon and tuna fish he had consumed throughout a long and well-regulated life. Charlie had no fears on the score of his Mass attendance record, either. He had never missed Mass on Sundays or holy days except on a few occasions when he was sick in bed. And even on those occasions he had been careful to confess that he had missed Mass, "just to be sure." Charlie had been a faithful user of his Sunday envelopes, too. He was confident that his generosity to the Church militant was duly recorded in the files of the Church triumphant.

"It all sounds so familiar," said a dull, flat voice. Charlie whirled around. He had not been aware that he was thinking out loud. He had not been aware, either, that anyone else was about. Then he saw the owner of the voice—an old man with a long white beard. He was dressed in a fur-trimmed silk robe that extended all the way to his sandaled feet. On his head he wore a white turban, and about his neck a gold chain. He looked for all the world like one of the figures in a Bible illustration, Charlie thought.

"Yes, you are right. You have heard of me," the bearded man said, as if he had read Charlie's thoughts. "I appeared in one of the parables of Jesus of Nazareth. I am the Pharisee who was immortalized by a visit I once made to the temple in Jerusalem." Immediately into Charlie's mind leapt a story he had heard long ago, about a Pharisee and a publican who went into a temple to pray. The Pharisee had thanked God that he was not like the rest of men—robbers, liars, adulterers, or even the publican. He had fasted often and given money to the temple. But the publican would not so much as lift up his eyes to Heaven, but kept beating his breast, and asking God to be merciful to him because he was a sinner.

Charlie saw the point, and he did not like it. This Pharisee was an unbeliever. He had refused to accept Christ. Who was he to compare himself to Charlie, a lifelong member of the one true Church of Jesus Christ?

Once again the Pharisee seemed to have read Charlie's thoughts. He shrugged. "Wait and see what the Lord has to say to you," he said. For the first time Charlie felt a slight stab of fear. "What did He say to you?" he asked a little anxiously. "Don't you know?" the old Pharisee said. "He told me that I had all the satisfaction I deserved from the way I lived on earth. 'Amen I say to you,' the Lord told me, 'you have already received your reward.' "

Charlie felt a stab again, but he quickly reassured himself. After all, the Pharisees were a pretty bad lot, quite different from himself. What could he have in common with a Pharisee? He was a Christian, and he had lived in the twentieth century. What is more—he had been a practical Catholic. He had not only gone to Mass every Sunday, he had been an usher at the eight o'clock Mass for years. Yes, he *had* been in the habit of ducking out for a smoke during the sermon, but after all, that was no sin; the sermon was not a principal part of the Mass. "All you have to catch under pain of mortal sin is the Offertory, the Consecration, and the Communion," Charlie often said.

Yes, Charlie had been very careful to keep all the rules—all the rules which bound under sin. "Is it a sin?" he was always asking himself. His aim was to save his soul by keeping all the rules. For Charlie, this is what religion meant. His had been a religion of laws and obligations. God, he figured, kept pretty exact records, and he was determined that his score would be up to par for salvation.

In short, Charlie was a legalist, one whose religion was a matter of external observance, nothing more. In this Charlie was like the Pharisees, even though, as he pointed out to himself in an attempt at reassurance, the Pharisees had lived a long time ago. They hadn't been around for almost two thousand years.

Charlie was right in one respect—the Pharisees as a sect disappeared long ago. Gone are the fur-trimmed robes and the turbans. But Pharisaism did not depart with them. The spirit of the Pharisees, the spirit against which Christ preached, is still very much with us. It shows up in many ways. Here are just a few of them.

A child says in confession, "My mother said that I should go ahead and eat the meat on Friday. Then I could go to confession on Saturday." The mother is not disturbed at the idea of sin, even serious sin. For her, mortal sin is simply a stain on the soul which can be easily removed by the legal procedure of "going to confession."

A man asks this question about the Lenten fast: "Father, would it be all right if I skipped dessert at my main meal and had a piece of cake or pie as a snack later at night?" The questioner is not concerned with the spirit of the Lenten fast. He is not thinking of the love and spirit of sacrifice which alone makes self-denial meaningful to God. He is preoccupied solely with the law of fasting and with the extent to which it binds him.

Says one of the mourners at a wake, "I'd like to receive Communion at the funeral tomorrow, but I can't unless I go to confession first, because I had the flu last Sunday and had to miss Mass." The lady thinks that one can somehow become guilty of mortal sin even when one does nothing wrong, that it is simply a legal penalty which one incurs for not fulfilling an obligation which one is not expected to fulfill under the circumstances.

All the above are examples of something which is the very spirit of Pharisaism—legalism. The Pharisees were greatly concerned with the Law. They were careful to keep it, down to the smallest detail. But they were so preoccupied with the letter of the Law that they lost sight of its spirit. They came to think that the mere external observance of the laws of God constituted holiness. Far from seeing the Mosaic Law as God intended it, as a means of showing love of God and grateful fidelity to His Covenant, the Pharisees saw it as an end in itself. Hence they dedicated their lives to a punctilious observance of the Law without bothering about the dispositions of their heart and soul. They made the critical mistake of assuming that God would judge a man to be holy merely because he was scrupulously exact about such things as dietary restrictions and ceremonial washings.

The Pharisaic sect had originated as a very praiseworthy movement to bring the Jewish people back to the full observance of God's Law. It degenerated into an empty formalism and ridiculous legalism which Jesus continually exposed and attacked. Our Lord's opposition was genuinely shocking to the Pharisees. Keeping the Law as they interpreted it was more important in their eyes than charity and the works of mercy; these men, who regarded swatting a fly as hunting and therefore an act which was forbidden on the Sabbath, were therefore deeply scandalized to see Jesus cure the sick on that day.

The height of absurdity to which their legalism led the Pharisees was evident on Good Friday. They did not hesitate to bribe false witnesses to testify at the trial of Jesus, and yet they would not dream of entering the house of Pilate, because to enter the house of a Gentile would have rendered them "legally unclean." They did not scruple to bring to a shameful death One Whom they knew to be innocent of any crime, and yet they were careful to see that His body was removed from the cross and that they were all in their homes by sundown, the beginning of the Sabbath, as the Law commanded. Such behavior strikes one as simply incredible. But is it really so different from that of today's dishonest politician who would not dream of eating meat on Friday? Legalism, in our modern day, can easily lead to such inconsistencies, just as it did in the time of the Pharisees.

It was not very difficult for the Pharisees to fall into legalism. Of necessity they were greatly concerned with the Mosaic Law, and the Law reached into every department of their lives. It was easy for their insistence on exact observance of the Law to degenerate into preoccupation with external observance and to lead them into the error of thinking that a rigid external observance of the Law was enough to satisfy God and accomplish their sanctification.

Catholics are faced with a similar danger, not so great a one as confronted the Pharisees but a real danger nevertheless. As children, Catholics are taught their prayers, taught the very words to say. It is easy to fall into the habit of assuming that the words themselves, muttered swiftly and without thought, constitute a good prayer. One can easily forget the old definition of prayer—the raising of the mind and heart to God—and act as if the prayer formula, the words of the prayer, worked automatically, *ex opere operato*, as the sacraments do.

The sacraments can be approached with this same kind of distortion. There is always the danger that one will come to use the sacraments of Penance and the Eucharist in a thoughtless and routine way, with little or no preparation, with little or no attempt to arouse in oneself the dispositions of heart and soul which are necessary for a really proper and fruitful reception of these sacraments. Catholics know that the sacraments work *ex opere operato*, that is, that they always have their effect when they are validly administered and when no obstacle is placed to the grace they give. This very fact can make people lazy and careless. They can come to rely too much on the objectivity of the sacraments and begin to treat them as if they were some sort of supernatural automatic machines.

This formalism can show up as legalism regarding the laws of the Church and the commandments. Catholics are trained from early childhood to take a serious view of their duty to assist at Mass on Sundays and holy days of obligation and to be very strict in the matter of Friday abstinence. Well and good. But some seem to equate these two laws of the Church with the Catholic life itself. They may have reasoned subconsciously that since Catholics are the only ones who do these things, these things themselves are the badge of a Catholic. They may even have come to regard them as the only things which make Catholics different from other people.

This was the attitude of one old man who came back to the sacraments after having been away for many years. He began his confession by saying, "Put me down for everything, Father." And sure enough, each question put by the priest was met with a sigh and a "Yes, many times" —each question, that is, except, "Have you ever eaten meat on Friday?" To this the old man replied with some indignation, "I may have been very bad, but I didn't give up my religion and become a Protestant." This was the attitude, too, of a man who was taking an examination for membership in the Knights of Columbus. When he was asked, "What are the two greatest commandments of the Law?" he did not give the expected answer, "Love God and love your neighbor." "Go to Mass on Sunday and don't eat meat on Friday," was his prompt reply.

When it comes to the ten commandments, once again, Catholics can easily show a legalistic bent. They have learned so many thou-shalt-nots that they can fall into the error of assuming that holiness consists simply in not doing things. They can adopt the philosophy of the three monkeys, "See no evil, hear no evil, speak no evil," and equate it with the Christian life. This is the attitude which is betrayed often enough by penitents who come to confession and say, "It has been six months since my last confession, and I haven't committed any sins in that time." No one wants a negative preoccupation with sin, but this attitude is also wrong. It reveals the fact that the penitent thinks that all that God expects from us is to refrain from breaking the commandments. The person who thinks this way would have a difficult time trying to understand why our Lord cursed the barren fig tree and caused it to wither away.

A legalistic cast of mind generates a false attitude toward the faith itself. Membership in the Church can come to mean merely being under the necessity of obeying all kinds of repressive laws and accepting without question a series of propositions. Faith is regarded as unquestioning intellectual fidelity, nothing more. The will must "toe the mark" and see to it that all the rules are kept, even those which seem very arbitrary. God is looked upon not as a loving Father but as a stern judge Who is forever testing our loyalty and obedience. The Christian life is thought to be a burdensome thing, no fun really, but a necessary discipline.

This attitude is a gross misrepresentation of the Catholic life. Actually, it is the Calvinistic concept of Christianity, not the Catholic. True, there are some stern souls who rather enjoy living according to this philosophy, satisfied with the feeling of righteousness which they get from a grim and joyless performance of duty. There are people who enjoy repressing themselves just as there are people who enjoy a plunge into icy waters in January. But these people are a decided minority. Many who have this distorted idea of the Christian life are not very happy about being Catholics. They wouldn't dream of changing and couldn't imagine being anything else, but they do not experience the joy which membership in the Church should bring them. When they hear or read about how happy the saints were, even in the midst of their afflictions, they either have deep doubts or simply conclude that saints are after all very odd people, quite different from everyone else.

But there are other legalistic-minded souls who are not so afflicted. They see the Church as an institution which imposes obligations upon them, but they find the burden light. They see the Christian life as the good life, full of comforts and pleasures and worldly preoccupations, no different from the kind of life lived by people who have no religion except that it entails keeping the commandments, going to Mass on Sunday, and abstaining from meat on Friday. Keeping the commandments, as these people see it, can be rather difficult at times, of course. "Thou shalt not commit adultery" presents problems, especially up to a certain age, but the other commandments are not very demanding. "Thou shalt not steal" means to them simply that they may not take other people's money.

They are blissfully unaware of any connection between this commandment and social or interracial justice or certain business practices, such as padding expense accounts, which "everybody does." For these people, "Love thy neighbor" means "Let him keep to himself and I'll keep to myself, and I won't do anything to hurt him." The aim of this type of Catholic is to live comfortably in this world and keep out of mortal sin in order to assure his salvation. Religion for him is a very simple thing. It is a matter of saying prayers and going to Church. It doesn't affect the way he acts in his business and social life. He merely fulfills his obligations and goes on living just as other people do; he has "the best of two worlds."

There are other Catholics who are affected by legalism but who do not fit into any of the groups described above. They genuinely love the Church and are wholehearted in their loyalty to her. They are neither unhappy about the restrictions which the laws of God and of the Church impose upon them nor content to regard the Church simply as a club which has its special by-laws. They sense that the Church has a life which is far deeper than the one they see on the surface. They have learned their catechism and know what the Church teaches; but they are dissatisfied with what they know. They feel that the truths of the faith have a more profound meaning than they have ever discovered, that there is much more to the Mass and the sacraments than they have learned in their catechism. They are haunted by the thought that the Christian life is deeper and fuller than they had always found theirs to be. These people sense that real happiness is to be found within their religion, but they know that this happiness is not to be found in merely keeping the commandments. These Catholics are really searching for the immense treasure which lies deep within the Church. To discover this treasure they must rid themselves of the sterile legalism which blinds them to the true nature of the Christian life.

Our Lord Jesus Christ did not come to promulgate laws; He came to call men to a new life, a joyful life, a life of intimacy with God. He came to draw men together into the family of God. His message might be summed up, "God is your Father. He loves you and wishes to give you eternal life. Love God and love each other as your Father loves you." When Jesus gave the apostles the commission to spread His Kingdom throughout the world, He sent them to preach the good news of salvation to all men. The joyful message, far from announcing a new set of rules and restrictions, proclaimed a new life of freedom, the freedom of the children of God. To the Christians at Ephesus, people who had formerly belonged to the class of "heathen Gentiles," strangers to the family of God, slaves to their vices and to the pagan practices to which their ignorance and their superstition led them, St. Paul wrote:

> . . . bear in mind that you were at that time without Christ, excluded as aliens from the community of Israel, and strangers to the covenants of the promise, having no hope, and without God in the world. But now in Christ Jesus you, who were once afar off, have been brought near through the blood of Christ. For he himself is our peace, he it is who has made both one, and has broken down the intervening wall of the enclosure, the enmity, in his flesh. The Law of the commandments expressed in decrees he has made void, that of the two he might create

in himself one new man and make peace and reconcile both in one body to God by the cross, having slain the enmity in himself. And coming, he announced the good tidings of peace to you who were afar off, and of peace to those who were near; because through him we both have access in one Spirit to the Father. Therefore, you are now no longer strangers and foreigners, but you are citizens with the saints and members of God's household. . . . [Eph 2:12–20]

The Christian life is not simply the adopting of new beliefs and principles; it is a completely new life. One does not "join" the Church, really; one is born into it. This was the truth which Jesus tried to convey to Nicodemus, the man who came to Him by night seeking information about the Kingdom. Standing in the shadows beside the Temple in the still night air, Nicodemus could hardly believe his ears. "Amen, amen I say to thee," Jesus said to him, "unless a man be born again, he cannot see the kingdom of God." This concept of being born for a second time was completely bewildering to Nicodemus. "How can a man be born when he is old?" he asked Jesus. "Can he enter a second time into his mother's womb and be born again?" Our Lord explained. Baptism was to be this new birth by which a man would receive the new life which Christ came to bring. "Amen, amen, I say to thee," Jesus said, "unless a man be born again of water and the Spirit, he cannot enter into the kingdom of God. That which is born of the flesh is flesh; and that which is born of the Spirit is spirit. Do not wonder that I said to thee, 'You must be born again.' The wind blows where it will, and thou hearest its sound but dost not know where it comes from or where it goes. So is everyone who is born of the Spirit" (Jn 3:3–8).

Baptism is a rebirth. This fact was made dramatically evident by the very rite of Baptism in ancient times. In those days the baptismal font was not an urn or a small receptacle but a pool. Three steps led into this pool, which contained the waters of Baptism, and three steps led out at the other side. The one to be baptized removed all his clothes before entering the pool. This action symbolized the putting off of his old pagan ways and habits. Then he entered the pool and walked to the center, where a deacon was waiting to baptize him. (In the case of women, deaconesses were used.) The one to be baptized was totally immersed in the water to symbolize the death and rebirth of the new Christian. He was dying to his old self; he was laying down his life symbolically, in imitation of Christ, Who in very fact laid down His life by dying on the cross. As the new Christian rose from waters of Baptism, he rose to a new life, as Christ rose on the first Easter morning. As a symbol of this new life which he had just received the newly baptized person was clothed in a pure white garment as he emerged from the pool. Thus was it brought home to him that he had died to sin, had buried his sins, as it were, in the waters of Baptism, and had been born again of water and the Spirit. He was truly born again, "born," as St. John tells us, "not of blood, nor of the will of the flesh, nor of the will of man, but of God." (Jn 1:13)

The baptismal font is not a pool nowadays. The significance of Baptism as a rebirth is not so dramatically portrayed as it once was. Yet the reality is the same. The newly baptized person looks exactly as he did before; there is no change in him as far as the human eye can see. But in the eyes of God there has been a tremendous change. Before, this person had been only the handiwork of God—a marvelous thing, to be sure, but merely a part of God's natural creation. He was greater than the other things of nature which God had made, the earth, the plants, and the animals, because he could know and he could love. But he could know God only as his Creator and his Master. He could love God only in the things God had made. Now he is a new creature; now he lives with the very life of God. Now he is no longer merely the handiwork of God; he is God's own son. Looking at him, God sees not merely a man, a creature of body and spirit. He sees His own Son, Jesus Christ. He sees one who is alive with the life of Christ. He sees one who can know Him now not merely as his Creator and Master but as his Father, who can respond to God's love and love Him in return.

There is a true story of an old lady who had a guppy. One day the old lady took a long, hard look at the guppy and became upset. There seemed to be something wrong with the fish. It wasn't taking its food. It was listless. Only a very determined guppy-lover, which the old lady was, could have noticed it—but the guppy was sick. The old lady tenderly picked up the fish bowl and carried the ailing guppy to a veterinarian. The veterinarian had had odd cases before, but this one easily took the prize. "Lady," he said, "you can buy those things for a penny in any pet store. Why don't you just throw this fish away and go get another one?" The old lady looked at the veterinarian with tears in her eyes. "Don't you understand?" she said. "This isn't just *any* guppy. This is *my* guppy."

This story may seem far-fetched, but it does bring out

one point—people value things and even love them when those things belong to them in a special way. Baptism makes a creature belong to God in a very special way, to a far greater extent than he belonged to God merely as His creature. He now belongs to God as a child belongs to his father.

Watch the faces of parents at a high-school graduation. They sit in polite boredom as one capped and gowned figure after another steps forward to receive a diploma. But suddenly they sit up. They are all attention. Their eyes light up. A smile breaks out on their faces. This particular capped and gowned figure that has just stepped forward is not just any capped and gowned figure. This is their own child. Such is the case with God, our Father. God loves everything which He has made, but the baptized Christian is a child of God and therefore the object of God's special, paternal love.

The story of the guppy may strike some as touching; it will strike most as silly. It is silly for anyone, even a lonely old lady, to love a guppy. The guppy is worthless and totally unworthy of being the object of love. But a human being, although far from worthless, is of himself unworthy of being the object of God's paternal love. Baptism actually brings about in a human being a change so profound that it renders him worthy of God's fatherly love. In the rebirth of Baptism God gives His creature a new life. This new life is nothing less than a sharing in the nature of God. It makes the baptized person holy in his very being. It causes him to become a living temple of God, one in whom the Blessed Trinity dwells lovingly.

It is said of the father of Origen, a prominent figure in

the early Church of Africa, that he knelt beside the crib of his newly baptized infant in adoration of the Blessed Trinity dwelling within the sleeping child. This may seem to be rather strange and unusual behavior, but it demonstrates a great fact—the profound holiness of the baptized Christian as one who literally bears God within himself. The Christian, cleansed by the redeeming blood of Jesus Christ, reflects the holiness of God Himself. He belongs to the all-holy God. He is God's property and possession. St. Paul, writing to the Corinthians, expresses this important truth: "Do you not know that your members are the temple of the Holy Spirit, who is in you, whom you have from God, and that you are not your own? For you have been bought at a great price. Glorify God and bear him in your body" (1 Cor 6:19–20).

St. Paul never tired of speaking about the holiness of the baptized Christian. In his letter to the Ephesians Paul wrote:

> Blessed be the God and Father of our Lord Jesus Christ, who has blessed us with every spiritual blessing on high in Christ. Even as he chose us in him before the foundation of the world, that we should be holy and without blemish in his sight in love. He predestined us to be adopted through Jesus Christ as his sons, according to the purpose of his will, unto the praise of the glory of his grace, with which he has favored us in his beloved Son. [Eph 1:3–6]

As soon as the deep, interior holiness of the baptized Christian is established, a necessary corollary is at once established. It is well expressed in a phrase often used in Scholastic philosophy—agere *sequitur* esse, meaning that the actions of any given being are in accordance with the nature of that being. In other words, birds act like birds, dogs act like dogs, human beings act like human beings. The application to the Christian is obvious. He has received a new life from God; he must now act according to that life. He has been made holy in his very being; now his actions must be holy. He has been made a son of God; now he must live and act as a son of God.

The first Christians in the community at Jerusalem were well aware that they were called upon to lead a new life since they had been baptized. They had been believers before; they had been Jews, God's people, and had always kept the Law and the commandments. But they were conscious now of a great difference. That difference was Jesus Christ. Hitherto they had tried to serve God by keeping His Law. It had been a Law, not a person, which bound them to God. But now God had come among them. God had come to them as a man, with a human heart and a human soul. It was now a person who united them to God, Jesus Christ, the God-man. Christ had fulfilled the Old Law and had given them a New Law. He had told them that they were to love one another.

But Jesus had not left this teaching vague and up in the air. He had told them that they were to love one another as *He had loved them.* They knew very well how He had loved them; He had laid down His life for them. Jesus had set no limits to the holiness which should distinguish his followers. "You therefore are to be perfect," He said, "even as your heavenly Father is perfect" (Mt 5:48). These words would have been meaningless before Christ came. How could one go about imitating the invisible God? But now the words had great meaning. Here was God, present among man in the God-man. Jesus had shown how the Son of God acts. He had spent His every minute loving and ministering to others. People had seen His mercy, His kindness, His love of the poor and the oppressed. They had seen His whole-souled devotion to His Father and His complete dedication to doing His Father's will.

"A new commandment I give you," Jesus had said, "that you love one another; that as I have loved you, you also love one another. By this will all men know that you are my disciples, if you have love for one another" (Jn 13:34-35). A Christian was to ask himself not "What does the Law say?" but "What would Christ do?" Love, not legal observance of rules, was to be the mark of a follower of Christ.

The modern Christian should live by the same standard as the earliest Christian. His model is nothing less than Jesus Christ Himself. Men will know that he is a disciple of Jesus Christ not by the regularity with which he goes to Church, not by his fidelity to laws of fasting and abstinence, not by his generous contributions to the Church, but by the love he shows for others.

Among the nobility in a bygone age the words *noblesse oblige* were very meaningful. These words expressed the idea that the nobleman's status obliged him to act in a way which was different from and superior to that which was expected of the common people. A peasant might quite properly take to his heels when confronted with a fellow peasant who was brandishing a knife; a nobleman was expected to stand his ground. His nobility required him to show bravery and courage.

Even in the absence of an aristocracy of blood, the idea of *noblesse oblige* still prevails to some extent. Those in public posts and professional people are expected to show more nobility than people in ordinary walks of life. Their lives are to be free from any taint of scandal. They are supposed to be a credit to their office or their profession. But it is in the case of the baptized Christian that *noblesse oblige* is most meaningful. The new life which the Christian receives in Baptism gives him a nobility incomparably greater than that which is founded on social status. If a higher standard of conduct is expected of the children of kings and presidents, how much more is to be expected of those who are children of God Himself?

The actions of a child always reflect on the parent. If Johnny jumps on the furniture and pulls the cat's tail while visiting a neighbor, everyone wonders what kind of people Johnny's mother and father are. If Johnny is well-behaved and says "please" and "thank you," everyone concludes at once that his parents are well-mannered. With the children of God it is the same. The actions of Christians actually have an influence on other people's attitudes toward God. The Christian is constantly on parade before the world. The world is watching and expecting to see a way of life which is different from that of the world. It is a well-known fact, too, that people form their opinion of the Church in most cases by observing Catholics rather than by reading books. Our Lord Himself tells all Christians of the importance of their good example: "You are the light of the world. A city set on a mountain cannot be hidden. Neither do men light a lamp and put it under the measure, but upon the lamp-stand, so as to give light to all in the house. Even so let your light shine before men, in order that they may see your good works and give glory to your Father in heaven" (Mt 5:14–16).

The legalist lets no light shine before men. Seeing him, people get a false and unappealing picture of the faith. The Catholic who finds in his religion nothing but burdens, rules, and restrictions gives the impression that the Christian life is a negative and gloomy business. Those who base their judgment of the Church on him are apt to think that Catholics are people who have to get up and go to Church every Sunday, who may not eat meat on Friday or practice birth control, who must submit their minds to the Church and form all their opinions according to what they are told, and who must do everything the Church tells them to do. The Catholic who sees the Christian life as merely the worldly life with a few added rules which make all the difference between salvation and damnation gives the impression that it is not worth bothering about. He leads others to think that Catholics are just like everybody else except that they go to Church on Sunday and don't eat meat on Friday.

What a different picture of the faith is given by one who truly appreciates it himself and lives it. It is not without reason that St. Francis of Assisi is so universally admired and loved. Even unbelievers feel his appeal. They cannot help being captured by his joy, his simplicity, his love. But what is so attractive about this saint is the true Christian spirit he displays, the spirit of the Gospel shining forth in him. This same spirit is to be found in all those who truly understand the faith and live the Christian life.

All the world loves a lover, it is said. In sum, love is what everything comes down to. The legalist is not a lover. He is not in love with God; he merely keeps rules. He is like the woman in prison, or like a wife who does not love her husband but keeps house for him and cooks his meals because it is her duty. She is not happy and she doesn't make those around her happy. But a true Christian is above all a lover. He keeps the rules, of course, but he sees these rules as important for only one reason—they are ways of showing love. The modern Pharisee is a "professional Christian." He knows all the rules and is expert at keeping them. The true Christian is an "amateur," in the root meaning of that word—one who is a Christian because he loves, and who sees the Christian life for what it is: a life of love.

2

Led by the Spirit

One of the first lessons a child learns is that there are a great many things he may not do. Again and again, as he reaches for an object, he hears, "No, no," or receives a light premonitory slap on the hand. He is told that he must not pick the flowers which belong to the people next door, or that he must not take Tommy's toy away from him. At first the child knows only that certain actions call forth a frown or a slap and that others bring a smile and a pat of approval. It is not until much later that he begins to realize that some actions are good and others are bad in what grown-ups call a moral sense. It is when a child reaches the stage where he is aware of moral good and evil that he comes to know what is called the natural law. He knows not only that he ought to do good and avoid evil but also in a general way what is good and what is evil. Even if he were not taught that it is wrong to lie and steal and be mean to others, he would eventually come to realize this himself. The child becomes aware that one of the big differences between himself and his dog lies in this sense of right and wrong. The dog goes on merely associating various actions with pleasure or pain, approbation or punishment; the child reaches the point where he realizes that there is a law which tells him how human beings are to act. If the child is fortunate, he will be taught the meaning of this law and will be shown how reasonable and necessary it is.

The all-wise Creator has put laws into everything He has made. The universe could not function without these laws. All would be utter chaos if the heavenly bodies did not keep to their regular courses. Life would be impossible if each plant and animal did not act according to the laws of its own nature. God has put these laws into the very elements. Water predictably boils and freezes, at the proper temperatures; chemicals unfailingly combine and separate according to their inherent properties. All objects are affected, according to their nature, by the laws of gravity, of acceleration and deceleration. Living things, too, come into being, grow, and act according to the laws of their natures. Birds build their nests, hatch and care for their young, and migrate generation after generation in exactly the same way. All the animals are guided by God-given instincts. These instincts are essential to their survival. They drive the animal to do and to avoid whatever he must do and avoid if he and his species are to live.

Man does not depend on instinct to the extent that animals do. God has given man a higher power to guide him. Man has a mind; he must discover what is good for him and what is bad. He must discover how a man is to live. Thus, a human being comes to see that there are certain laws which are basic for human life, which are necessary for life on a human level, just as the laws of nature are necessary for life to exist on earth. This is what a child discovers when he becomes aware of moral values—that there is such a thing as good, which is to be done, and evil, which is to be avoided. This is what is called the natural law.

All men know this law, though their conceptions of what is good or evil here and now vary considerably. The ancient Romans, like some modern Japanese, regarded suicide as a good act, as a means of avoiding disgrace. In the Solomon Islands, headhunters saw nothing wrong in collecting the heads of people from another tribe; they thought it immoral to cut off the head of a fellow tribesman. One anthropologist tells of a noble chief who showed his respect for his parents in a way which to him seemed quite moral and proper. When the parents had grown too old to enjoy life, the chief arranged for a neighboring tribe to kill them and eat them; then he gave the bones an honorable burial. Among the Eskimos and certain African tribes a man shows hospitality to a visitor by sharing his wife with him, considering this practice to be perfectly moral. However, for a man to take another man's wife without the husband's consent would be considered very wrong and worthy of serious punishment.

These aberrations really show not a lack of moral sense but the very opposite. All men are conscious of a moral order and of a basic morality which should govern human actions. All men, of whatever civilization, know that it is wrong to lie and to steal and to take human life under certain circumstances. All men know that there is some kind of sexual morality. In other words, all men, even though they may never have heard of the Bible, know in some general form what we call the ten commandments. These commandments are a statement of the basic laws which flow from man's very nature and which are necessary for human life.

All men come to know these commandments in a natural way. Those who accept the Bible as the inspired word of God know them as moral laws which have been revealed by God. They are natural insofar as they express the natural law; they are supernatural in the sense that they were given by God himself to the people through Moses.

A young child might be pardoned for thinking of the ten commandments as arbitrary laws which God has made in order to test us. For an adult to think this way would be childish in the extreme. These commandments (with the exception of the third, which designates a special day of the week as the Lord's day) are not laws God has "enacted," really. They are laws which, far from being arbitrary, spring from the very nature of man, and which God has made clearly known to us. They spell out the way a man must live because he is a man. They enumerate the duties that man has toward God and toward his fellow man, duties that flow from human nature itself, and they protect man's natural rights.

This fact is basic to human freedom. It is the basis of the American Constitution. The founding fathers recognized that all men are created by God and that their basic human rights are given to them by God, not by the state. They realized more specifically that the commandments forbid men to violate the rights which other men have as human beings. Adolf Hitler refused to admit that man has any rights by nature. He had to, in order to justify his actions.

According to Hitler, what rights a man had were given to him by the state and could be taken away by the state; there were no ten commandments, no "thou shalt not kill" for this man who could send his troopers into a hospital in Poland with orders to machinegun in their beds all the sick men, women, and children. The Communists do not recognize the ten commandments. Neither can anyone who wants to justify tyranny and oppression and the denial of human rights.

Impatient with restraint, people sometimes half-wish that there were no ten commandments. How foolish such a wish is should be immediately apparent. A man might want to see the commandments repealed for a single day. He might make careful plans for all that he would do, innocently and with impunity, on that day. He might plan to kill the fellow down the street whom he dislikes intensely. He might decide to appropriate the Cadillac which belongs to the man next door. He might have ideas of running off with another man's wife. But on the day in question he would surely find that things would not work out as he had planned. Before he could get to the Cadillac, someone would very likely have driven off in his Ford. One of the neighbors might well have designs on his wife. It could even happen that there is someone in the block who dislikes him intensely and has every intention of shooting him first thing in the morning.

Actually, all adults realize that the commandments work both ways. If they forbid me to harm others, they forbid others to harm me. Even criminals are in favor of the ten commandments—that is, they are in favor of other people keeping them; a bank robber would refer to his partner in crime who ran off with all the loot as "that dirty crook." If man is commanded to worship God, man also has a very deep need to worship God, even though many people nowadays do not recognize that need for what it is. If man is commanded to respect the rights of all men, he has a need to live in community with other men, in a human world, a world where natural rights and duties are exercised in common.

The ancient Israelites knew the natural law before God gave them the ten commandments through Moses in the desert. They knew, as all men do, that good is to be done and evil avoided. What God gave them on Mt. Sinai was a clearer, more refined, more explicit knowledge of the natural law. Moreover, He gave them the Law as a bond between Himself and them, for the Mosaic Law, of which the ten commandments were the basic part, was the bond of the Covenant which God made with His people. The Israelite gloried in the fact that he was bound to God by this Law. He knew at every moment what was expected of him; it was all there in the Law.

There are Catholics today who expect an external guideline like the Law in the Old Testament. They want to be told what to do and what not to do. They take as their norm of perfection the ten commandments, and they are forever trying to apply them to their daily lives. These people do not understand the meaning of the Christian life, and have not really grasped the message of Christ. Theirs is essentially an Old Testament morality. They have not heard the words of St. Paul:

> But before the faith came we were kept imprisoned under the Law, shut up for the faith that was to be revealed. Therefore the Law has been our tutor unto Christ, that we might be justified by faith. But now that faith has come, we are no longer

under a tutor. For you are all the children of God through faith in Christ Jesus. For all you who have been baptized into Christ have put on Christ. . . .

But if you are led by the Spirit, you are not under the Law. [Gal 3:23–27, 5:18]

St. Paul says that Christians are not "under the Law." Is he saying, then, that Christians do not have to keep the ten commandments? Obviously not; common sense would tell us that. But St. Paul makes the point abundantly clear. Speaking of the new life which Christians are called upon to live, he says:

Wherefore, put away lying and speak truth each one with his neighbor, because we are members of one another. "Be angry and do not sin"; do not let the sun go down upon your anger: do not give place to the devil. He who was wont to steal, let him steal no longer, but rather let him labor, working with his hands at what is good, that he may have something to share with him who suffers need. Let no ill speech proceed from your mouth, but whatever is good for supplying what fits the current necessity, that it may give grace to the hearers. And do not grieve the Holy Spirit of God, in whom you were sealed for the day of redemption. Let all bitterness, and wrath, and indignation, and clamor, and reviling, be removed from you, along with all malice. On the contrary, be kind to one another, and merciful, generously forgiving one another, as also God in Christ has generously forgiven you. . . .

But immorality and every uncleanness or covetousness, let it not even be named among you, as becomes saints; or obscenity or foolish talk or scurrility, which are out of place; but rather thanksgiving. For know this and understand, that no fornicator, or unclean person, or covetous one (for that is idolatry) has any inheritance in the kingdom of Christ and God. [Eph 4:25–5:5]

In these words St. Paul certainly says that Christians must observe the ten commandments; what, then, does he mean by saying that Christians are no longer "under the law"? Were not the ten commandments part—in fact, the basic part—of the Old Law? Actually, what St. Paul means is that while Christians must of course observe the ten commandments, as did the Jews and as must all men, the Christian life is not circumscribed by the ten commandments. He is saying that the norm of morality for the Christian is not the ten commandments but something beyond. The Christian is bound to God not by the Law, as were the Jews, but by a person, Jesus Christ. While the Christian observes all the precepts of the basic moral law, he looks for guidance and inspiration not to that law but to the Holy Spirit, dwelling within him and fashioning him in the image of Christ. In short, St. Paul's meaning is that what is expected of the Christian is Christian maturity, a maturity which could never have been achieved or even expected under the Old Law, before the coming of Christ.

In order really to understand a man it is necessary to know something of his childhood. It is necessary to see the factors which contributed to his development and to trace that development through its various stages. Biographies always speak first of the parents of the subject of the book, and then proceed to describe his childhood. So it is with the story of God's family. God's family today is in the stage of adulthood. It is the Body of Christ; it is the fullness of Christ. While it is awaiting its ultimate perfection and is continuing to grow, it has already come to maturity. The family of God lives today in the "last days of this world." The first days, the early days, the centuries and centuries of groping, the ages which saw man's slow and painful development toward a deeper relationship with God are all behind. The final glory, the final union of the beatific vision itself, still lies ahead, but the family of God today is united to God through Christ in the intimacy of fatherhood and sonship. God can and does expect a response which He could not expect before. He can and does expect of each Christian that he will come to full maturity as a Christian. But in order to achieve this maturity the Christian must understand what he is. He must know his own spiritual ancestry. He must see the family of God as it was in the beginning.

It is easy to feel irritation when reading the Old Testament. The people were so fickle, so unreasonable, so undependable, so downright "cussed" at times. God was so patient with them and so merciful, and yet they were always ready at the drop of a hat to turn aside from Him and run off to worship idols. Again and again God came to their rescue—He fed them and took care of all their wants—and still at the first hardship they grumbled and complained and carried on as if God had never done anything for them. God gave them victory in battle, and they showed their gratitude by turning away from Him and adopting the abominable practices of their pagan neighbors. "How could God put up with these people?" one might well wonder. "Why did he forgive them again and again when they acted like irresponsible children?" The answer, of course, lies ultimately in the infinite mercy of God, but there is another consideration, too. These people acted like children because morally and religiously they were children. God expected no more of them than one would expect from children, for the family of God at that time was in its infancy.

God had made preparations for the founding of His

family by calling Abraham and by guiding the destinies of Isaac and Jacob and his family. But the family of God was really born, one might say, at Mt. Sinai, when God said to the Hebrews, who were gathered about the foot of the mountain, "I will be your God; you will be My people." God alone knows His reason for choosing this small group of loosely related, seminomadic tribes which had recently fled from slavery in Egypt as the recipients of His Covenant. But one thing is certain: they did not choose God; it was God Who chose them.

The Covenant which God entered into with the Hebrews was expressed in terms similar to those of the treaties made in those days between a king and his vassals. The treaty imposed obligations on the vassals but none on the king. The king, on his part, promised to care for and protect his vassals, provided they kept their part of the agreement. So it was that God, in His Covenant, bound the Hebrews by the ten commandments and the other prescriptions of the Mosaic Law, in turn promising that if the Hebrews kept His Law, He would protect them, cherish them, give them a land of their own, and be with them always, in war and peace.

In order to understand the Old Law it is necessary to bear in mind how primitive and undeveloped the Hebrew people were at this early stage of their history. By comparison with their pagan contemporaries they were far advanced in a religious sense, to be sure, but by comparison with us they were in a state of religious infancy. They had revelations from God, but these were only gleams of light compared to the bright sunshine of God's full revelation which we enjoy. God revealed Himself to them only very slowly and gradually, as befitted their capacity to absorb His revelation. They did not have the understanding of God and of His plan of salvation that we have, they did not have the sacraments, and most important, they did not have Christ as their model, teacher, and sanctifier. God was invisible, a presence in the tent that was His dwelling. He was a God Who made His will known through patriarchs and prophets, not a God they could see with their eyes or hear with their own ears. They did not even have any images, any pictures or statues of any kind, of this God. Now that God has become man He has become visible in the sense that we can picture Him in the man Jesus Christ. When we look at Christ, it is God we are looking at—God in human form. Christ gives us His words, His example to guide us in our daily life and His Spirit to dwell within us.

The Hebrews did not have these incomparable advantages. It was necessary, therefore, for God to spell out in great detail how these people were to act if they were to be His children. Just as parents must be very explicit and comprehensive in their instructions to small children, so God had to explain to the Hebrews even the smallest matters which were involved in their religious lives. The will of God is encountered not in the abstract but in concrete acts and situations; if they were to know the will of God for them in all the situations which arose in daily life, God would have to tell them. And God did tell them, in His law. Then, too, since the Hebrews belonged to God, everything they possessed belonged to God also—their bodies, their time, their land, their possessions. The Law, therefore, covered every aspect of the life of the people. There were laws governing man's moral conduct—the ten commandments.

There were what might be called civil laws; since it was God Who ruled His people, even the laws which regulated their social, economic, and political life had His sanction. There were laws about the worship of God—about the tabernacle, the feasts, the offering of sacrifice, and the ministers of the temple. There were laws regulating religious observances, such as the laws which distinguished between "clean" and "unclean" animals.

Some idea of the breadth of the Law and the extent to which it penetrated every part of the life of the people can be obtained from a cursory reading of the books of Exodus, Leviticus, Deuteronomy, and Numbers. It is not to be thought, however, that the full Law, with all its refinements and ramifications, was given by God to Moses in the desert. God gave the basic Law through Moses in the form of the ten commandments and various regulations. These regulations were developed as the centuries went by. Moses himself added many regulations, drawing on his knowledge of Egyptian law. Later, when the Hebrews came into contact with the Assyrians and the Babylonians, who had an advanced system of law, they adopted some of the juridical practices of these people and incorporated them into Mosaic Law. Many prescriptions had their origin in the customs of the people. The rules governing hospitality in the Mosaic Law, for instance, were common among all the nomadic tribes of the East. Father Albert Gelin, P.SS., has this to say about the heterogeneity of the Mosaic Law:

> A surprise awaits anyone who examines the text in which the rules for Israel's conduct are laid down. In the midst of moral precepts appear commands which have nothing to do with ethics. Numerous sexual taboos (Lev 15:16–24, 12: 2), rules governing

contacts with corpses and lepers, prohibitions about food and eating food—various taboos of the sort that we encounter in a primitive civilization. Sociologists often introduce modern preoccupation, especially hygiene, into their explanation of these pointless regulations. In general, it is fair to say that they form a brake on a number of instinctive impulses and bear witness to the discipline which was perhaps the earliest aspect of morality. By welcoming them and changing them into commandments, the Bible once more performs its function of forming a link with the oldest human society. In spite of the tendency, especially in Deuteronomy, to rationalize taboos, the fact remains that their arbitrary nature enables Israel to appreciate more clearly the austerity of God's leadership. As Franz Rosenzweit puts it, "Do not say: I do not like pork; I like it very much, but my Father in heaven has forbidden me to partake of it."*

What is important to remember is that whatever the origin of the various regulations of the Mosaic Law, the Law as such was of divine origin. The later additions and elucidations were always attributed to Moses and given his authority, and Moses was God's spokesman. The book of Deuteronomy, compiled and given its present form about the year 600 B.C., six hundred years after the death of Moses, attributes all its legislation to him. When questions arose as to how these laws were to be applied in a particular case, men called Scribes, who were experts in the Law, would make decisions. In time the decisions of the Scribes acquired the same force as the original laws. In any event, it was universally recognized that the whole Law was God's and that its purpose was to bind the Hebrews to God and direct their lives to the better service of God. The great contribution of the ancient Hebraic Law was that it gave

*Father Albert Gelin, P.S.S., *The Religion of Israel* (New York, 1959), pp. 41–42.

men to understand, for the first time in history, that laws were not merely the means by which men lived at peace with one another, but also the means by which men lived at peace with God and showed their love for Him.

The history of Israel is the history of a people who were described by God Himself as "stiff-necked." It is a story of repeated infidelity to God and to His Covenant. Each time the people were unfaithful they were punished by God. The worst of these punishments came in the sixth century before Christ, when the Babylonians conquered the kingdom of Judah, destroyed Jerusalem, and led the Israelites as captives into Babylon. To all appearances this was the end of the chosen people. In reality it was the occasion of a great revival of faith and fervor, which bore fruit in the remnant of the people who returned to their own country in 539 B.C.

Living in exile in a pagan land, the Israelites were forced to come to grips with reality. Many fell away, of course, and abandoned all practice of their religion, but others reacted to the pagan environment in which they lived by becoming more religious. Back in their own country, surrounded by all the familiar trappings of their religion, many of the people had given only lip service to God; there had been widespread immorality and general disregard for the Law. In Babylon, far away from the Temple, the captive Israelites began to realize the true meaning of their religion. They had come to regard the political entity which was the kingdom as the bond which united them as a people. With the kingdom dissolved, they realized that it was their religion which bound them together and set them apart from all other people. The men who came forward to lead the people during this period of exile were the priests. They gathered the people together for prayer and saw to it that the people were instructed in their faith. Most important, they brought about a revival of respect for the Law. The Law, which at home had been looked upon as a rather meaningless relic of antiquity, now was seen as a vital thing, and the observance of the Law became the mark of a good Jew.

Difficult as these years of exile were, they were years in which the people of God began to mature religiously. At home they had thought of God in a rather local and limited way. He was *their* God, and He was present in the temple at Jerusalem. Now they became more deeply aware of the fact that this God Who was their God was the only God, the God of Heaven and earth and of all things, present everywhere. Never again would these people be tempted to lapse into idolatry in any form, as their ancestors had done so often during their history.

When the Jews returned to their own country after the exile, they set about to rebuild the Temple and to practice their religion faithfully. But this happy state of affairs did not last long; once again a religious decline set in. This time, however, it took the form not of disregard for the Mosaic Law but, quite to the contrary, of exaggerated observance, which led to legalism and formalism. The Pharisees were most to blame. Their original zeal degenerated into cold rigorism. They made so many distinctions and subdivisions in the Law that they rendered its observance excessively difficult. They made it an intolerable burden, and at the same time they insisted that the people observe it down to the least detail. Precisely on this point Jesus upbraided the Pharisees. He accused them of placing unbearable strictures on the people by their unreasonable interpretations of and additions to the Law. Our Lord refused to accept the Pharisees' interpretations and thus incurred the hatred of those powerful leaders. He insisted that God's Law was a reasonable law. He reminded the people that the purpose of the Law was to bind them to God, and that the first and all-important precepts were those which obliged a man to love God with his whole heart and soul and to love his neighbor as himself.

Jesus scandalized the Pharisees by refusing to go along with their ridiculous interpretations, but He was completely faithful to the real Law. In His own words, He came not to destroy the Law but to fulfill it. He kept the Law because the Law was God's will, and He came to do His Father's will in all things. But in fulfilling the Law Christ transformed it. He did not abolish the Law, any more than nature abolishes a child by having him grow into a man. The Old Law had regulated men's external actions. To be sure, the people were supposed to keep it as a sign of their love for and fidelity to God, but interior thoughts and desires were not emphasized by the Law as Jesus emphasized them. Quoting the Old Law, Christ said:

> You have heard that it was said to the ancients, "Thou shalt not kill." . . . But I say to you that everyone who is angry with his brother shall be liable to judgment. . . .
>
> You have heard that it was said to the ancients, "Thou shalt not commit adultery." But I say to you that anyone who so much as looks with lust at a woman has already committed adultery with her in his heart. [Mt 5:21–22, 27–28]

Jesus transformed the imperfect Old Law into a new way of life, stressing holiness of mind and heart, requiring love and forgiveness of enemies, and prescribing imitation of the holiness of God Himself. In place of the Law, an external, temporary, and imperfect thing, our Lord gave Himself as the living exemplar and sanctifier and sent the Holy Spirit to dwell within us forever. Jesus brought the family of God to maturity. The Mosaic Law is unnecessary for the Christian, just as a tutor becomes unnecessary when a child has grown up.

Before Christ, members of the family of God were children in bondage under the Law, as St. Paul says. The Christian, with the full revelation of Jesus Christ and the new life which Christ has given him in Baptism, has been made adult and set free by Christ. Before Christ, men could only look forward to the coming Redeemer. Even the chosen people were part of a sinful, fallen race. God gave them the Law as a means of helping them toward holiness. The Law did not have within itself the power to make men holy; it merely showed them God's will and thereby guided them in their efforts to do that will. But the Christian is a "new creature," having been born again of water and the Spirit to a new life. He is united with Christ and lives with the life of Christ. He does not need the external Law as a guide to help him become holy; he has been made holy by Christ and he has the Holy Spirit to guide him in living the Christ life. Jacques Maritain has expressed it very well. He observes that whereas the moral precepts of the Old Law were for sinful men, teaching them how to be good and to become something which they were not, the doctrine of Christ and His precepts are for men who have been made holy by Christ and tells them how to remain holy, how to keep from falling back into a state of sin and slavery.

Moreover, Christ does more than make men holy in Baptism and teach them how to remain holy. He does more, even, than give Himself as the perfect examplar of holiness and His Law of Love as the law for the Christian. He gives Himself, quite literally, in the Eucharist as the very means of growth in holiness. He gives His grace, which enables the Christian to act as a child of God. He gives His Spirit, the Holy Spirit, to change the mind and heart of the Christian into the mind and heart of Christ.

As we said earlier, the Christian who seeks a law as his guideline is living according to Old Testament morality. Such a person does not have the Christian maturity which should be his as a member of the Body of Christ. The question he asks himself is not "How do I love?" but "Is it a sin?" He feels himself bound by laws much as the ancient Hebrew was. Often he feels that it is somehow sinful when he breaks these laws by accident. This is the kind of person, as we described him above, who feels that he must confess missing Mass on Sunday even though he was in bed with a fever of 103 degrees. This is the kind of person who feels that sin can be retroactive: he performs an action in all innocence—eating meat on Friday thinking it is Thursday, for example—and later, when it dawns on him that he has unknowingly broken the law, he thinks that he has become guilty of sin. Sin for him is a matter of breaking laws, and virtue a matter of keeping them.

The mature Christian knows that sin is not merely a matter of breaking a law but is also a failure to love. God is offended not because I ate meat on Friday but because by eating meat on Friday I showed that I did not love Him. God is offended not because I hurt my neighbor's feelings (I could have done so by accident, and God would not be offended at all) but because by hurting my neighbor's feelings I showed that I did not love him as God wants me to. The mature Christian knows that mortal sin is not merely a "stain on the soul" but a rejection of God, a refusal to love God, a clear-cut preference of something else to my Father, a breaking of my friendship with God. He realizes that mortal sin is horrible not because the action which is done is in itself horrible but because it is a refusal to love God—either directly or by a refusal to love one's neighbor. The mature Christian realizes also that venial sin is not a trivial thing; it is a failure to love God or one's neighbor as perfectly as a Christian should. Above all, the mature Christian knows that living the Christian life is not merely a matter of keeping out of sin. He understands the words of St. Augustine: "Love God, and do what you will." Like Christ, he is concerned simply with doing God's will at all times and with doing it because he loves God.

Here a very important question arises: how does one know what God's will is? The ancient Hebrews had the Law. This was a clear manifestation of God's will for them. But since the Christian is no longer under the Law, how is he to know what God expects of him at every moment? Some Catholics, genuinely and sincerely seeking to know God's will, look to the Church for the answer of even the tiniest question. They are forever asking what the Church says about a particular book or movie or what stand the Church takes on this or that controversial matter. It is true, of course, that the Church is Christ, teaching and guiding us, and that she does give us not only the principles of morality but also the counsels of prefection. But the Church can provide only the general principles. She cannot apply these principles to the many situations which arise in the daily life of her children. She teaches us to make these applications ourselves, acting according to our own conscience. But how is a Christian to form his conscience? How is he to know the will of God in individual instances? Here precisely is where the question of Christian maturity arises.

In place of the Law, the ancient Hebrew's exterior guide, the Christian has a guide that is within him, the Holy Spirit. The Holy Spirit lives and *acts* within the Christian, and His actions have one purpose—to make this member of Christ perfect as his heavenly Father is perfect, to form Christ in him, so that he may say with St. Paul, "It is no longer I that live, but Christ lives in me" (Gal 2:20).

The Holy Spirit, the Spirit of Jesus, led Jesus Himself. St. Matthew says that after His baptism, "Jesus was led into the desert by the Spirit, to be tempted by the devil" (Mt 4:1). Christ, it must never be forgotten, was a man, and as a man He grew in holiness by following the promptings of the Spirit within Him. In all things He did the will of His Father, and it was the Holy Spirit within Jesus Who told Him the will of His Father at every moment.

Good people are sometimes puzzled when they hear that they should imitate Christ. Jesus had no place to lay His head. He owned nothing. He went about doing good during His public life, preaching, teaching, and curing the sick. He did not get on a bus every day and go to work in an office. "How am I to imitate Christ?" these people ask. "Am I to stop playing golf? Shall I cancel my insurance? Shall I give up my automobile?" Their perplexity arises from a misconception of what it means to imitate Christ. The Christian is not expected to imitate the actions of our Lord literally, to adopt the mode of living of a different time and place, but rather to be guided in all things by the Holy Spirit as Jesus was. The saints lived lives which were very different from that of our Lord in particular circumstances, and yet they all imitated Christ and became Christlike. They, like Jesus, were led by the Spirit.

Too many people think of conscience as that still, small voice within a man which tells him merely what is right and wrong, what is sinful or not sinful. Actually, the conscience should do a great deal more than that. The Holy Spirit lives within a man not merely to make him moral but also to summon him to respond to the love of God, which has united him to the Blessed Trinity and given him a share in Its life. The Christian, hearing the summons, discovers the will and purposes of his loving Father in many things. He sees it in the ten commandments and in the laws of the Church, of course. But he sees it as well in the interior prompting of grace by which the Holy Spirit endeavors to lead him to greater holiness. One who understands this all-important fact is not preoccupied with the minimal requirements of the ten commandments and the laws of the Church, since he keeps the spirit as well as the letter and in his love for God goes beyond the laws. The legalist, on the other hand, looks for the widest latitude and still feels himself constantly restricted. The mature Christian sees the ten commandments for what they are—laws which "protect the outer periphery of the realm in which Christ will be formed in us." He does not make the mistake of seeing them as the only manifestation of God's will.

The word law must be clearly understood. On the one hand, St. Paul says that we are not "under the Law." On the other, he tells us that the Law is within us. In the first instance Paul is stating, as we have pointed out, that Mosaic Law is no longer binding. Yet he is not teaching that Christians may reject the ten commandments; that part of the Law—the moral precepts, as distinct from the legal and ceremonial precepts—is still binding on all men. The commandments, as we have seen, are part of natural law, which flows from human nature itself and is therefore necessary and irrevocable.

When St. Paul speaks of the Law which is within us, he is speaking not of the ten commandments but of the Holy Spirit, our divine Guide, and of the promptings of grace by which He leads us. A man may choose not to follow the Law in this sense and still commit no sin. Virginity, freely chosen for love of God, is more pleasing to God than marriage. Yet one who feels called to the religious life may choose not to follow the call and to marry without being guilty of any sin. It is always dangerous to confuse what God prompts us to do in order to please Him more with what we are obliged to do under pain of sin. That way lies fanaticism. Some years ago a priest expressed the opinion in a pamphlet that indulgence in alcohol and tobacco was not in keeping with the spirit of self-denial which Christ taught. Whatever the merit of his opinion, he was very wrong in the conclusion to which he jumped from there: he immediately went on to denounce all who drank or smoked, even in moderation, as sinners.

The Christian who is concerned only with keeping out of mortal sin will save his soul if he achieves his objective. When the rich young man asked Jesus what he needed to do in order to possess eternal life, our Lord told him simply to keep the commandments. But when the young man expressed the desire to go farther to strive for real holiness, Christ told him to follow Him. It goes without saying that our Lord expects His followers to keep the commandments. It is equally clear that He expects a great deal more. The will of God, He said, is our sanctification.

Moral theology is necessary. Priests must study it; all must have some knowledge of it. It is necessary to know the difference between right and wrong and the nature of mortal and venial sin. Moral theologians are quite rightly careful not to exaggerate sins, not to judge too severely. Priests hearing confessions should also be merciful in their judgments on the seriousness of sins. Everyone should have a correct conscience, not one which finds sin where there is none or finds mortal sin where there is only venial. This mistake is to stop there, to make moral theology the norm for living the Christian life rather than simply the norm for judging the sinfulness of an act.

The Christian conscience should be a wonderfully sensitive thing, so sensitive as to be able to perceive the gentle promptings of the Holy Spirit. The conscience of the mature Christian tells him when it would be sinful for him to act, that is, his conscience tells him that this act is commanded or forbidden by God. But he also knows when God is speaking to his conscience, endeavoring to lead him to greater holiness. A man's conscience may tell him he is smoking too much. The fanatic or scrupulous person reacts by saying to himself, "I am committing mortal sin by smoking too much." The legalist says, "It is not a sin, so why worry?" The mature Christian says, "Even though it is not a question of sin, wouldn't God be better pleased if I practiced temperance in this matter?"

A humorous picture once appeared on the cover of a Catholic magazine. It showed a monk in his simple brown habit and sandals walking blithely through a men's clothing store. On all sides were high-priced items—sport jackets, fancy shirts, jeweled cufflinks. The monk couldn't have cared less. He was pictured walking calmly along, looking straight ahead, with a smile on his face which could only be described as beatific. The caption under the picture was, "Freedom from want." This was more than a clever play on words; it underscored an important truth: a man who is free from the need to keep up with the Joneses is relieved of a great burden. He is truly free.

So it is with the mature Christian. He is truly free. Since he desires always to do the will of God, he does not do what others do or what he feels he *has* to do, but what he really wants to do. He is free from the inner conflict which many feel who try to compromise. He is free from the endless preoccupation with rules and laws which plagues the legalist. The legalist serves God as a hired servant serves his master. He does his job because it is his job. He does it for pay; he expects payment for services rendered. But the mature Christian acts toward God as a loving son toward his Father. He serves God because he loves Him. He looks forward not to a reward for services rendered but to eternal union with his Father as the fulfillment of his love. The mature Christian, therefore, is free from the spirit of servitude. His is the freedom of a son of God.

3

Faith: Our Response to God

On Chicago's near north side there is a little patch of green in the midst of all the asphalt and stone and concrete which everyone calls Bughouse Square. There on summer evenings, in accordance with an old tradition, soapbox orators hold forth. One of these, back in the 1930s, was a zealous young Catholic layman. Night after night this apostolic young man would mount his soapbox, and in a voice which he strove to make louder than those of the Communists and the pacifists and the advocates of everything from a soak-the-rich tax policy to the adoption of Esperanto, he would endeavor to refute various philosophies which are incompatible with Catholic belief.

One night, as often happened, he was interrupted by a heckler. "You told us what these other guys believe," the man shouted, "this guy Kant and this guy Spinoza. How about you? What do you believe?" The young speaker reacted immediately. He held his head high, and in a voice even louder than he had previously been using he shouted, "I believe in God, the Father almighty, Creator of heaven and earth." Then he proceeded to recite all the rest of the Apostles' Creed. The heckler was not impressed. "This guy ain't tellin' us what he believes," he complained. "He's prayin'." But the speaker was satisfied that he had given a clear, succinct presentation of the principal articles of faith.

In a sense, of course, the speaker was right. He had told what he believed—that is, he had enumerated the truths to which his intellect gave assent. He had done what most Catholics would have done under the circumstances. But in another sense the speaker was not right. He may have answered the question which had been asked; he told what he believed. But he did not tell the questioner what he really wanted and certainly needed to know: what faith is.

The answer which the young soapbox apostle gave was in accordance with the old catechism definition of faith: the assent of the mind to all the truths which God has revealed on the authority of God. The trouble is that this definition does not give the full meaning of faith. It was formulated at a time when the Church was combating errors which attacked the intellectual content of faith. Therefore, the Church used a definition which stressed the fact that faith is an intellectual acceptance of God's revelation and of each and every truth contained in the revelation. But this definition does not tell us what faith really is.

"I am the Lord thy God . . . . Thou shall not have strange gods before me" (Ex 20:2–3), God told the Hebrews. This, the first of the ten commandments, is by far the most important because it concerns that most important matter, faith. To refuse faith, to refuse to believe, to entertain deliberate doubts about anything which is a matter of faith would be a very serious sin against the first commandment. All Catholics know that they must believe everything the Church teaches. What some fail to realize, however, is that faith also means a wholehearted acceptance, an acceptance by the whole man, of a Being Who is truth itself, God. Faith involves more than the mind. It involves the whole person. And it is concerned with something more than cold facts, something more than mere statements of truths. It is concerned with a living Being, God, Who is not only truth itself but also love.

The mature Christian lives by faith. He is a man who has accepted God, who has made a commitment of himself to God. The mature Christian is first of all a man with a mature faith, a faith which has developed and grown and deepened under the influence of the grace of God and the action of the Holy Spirit. The faith of a mature Christian is a far cry from that of the child who recites and accepts each article of the Apostles' Creed. It is a far cry from the faith of one who is concerned only with "keeping the first commandment." It is something warm and living. It permeates the whole man. It involves a deep intimacy with God which colors every thought and action. It is the foundation and inspiration of the Christian's whole life.

Faith begins with God and comes only from God—the knowledge we have of God through faith is the knowledge God gives us of Himself. God has spoken. He has revealed Himself to man. He has revealed Himself not by enunciating a series of truths about Himself but by showing us His activity in history. God gives us His word. First He gave us His written word in the inspired pages of Holy Scripture. In the fullness of time He gave us His Word made flesh, Jesus Christ, Who is the "brightness of his glory and the image of his substance" (Heb 1:3), Who, man though He is, can say, "He who sees me sees also the Father" (Jn 14:9).

The message of faith, the Christian message, is the "proclamation of the salvation wrought by God in Christ and offered to all men who repent and believe." When it proclaims salvation it is telling a history, making known the mighty deeds of God. It announces the new order brought about by Jesus Christ. It calls men to repent of their sins and to turn to God, accepting Him with their whole being.

To appreciate the message of God it is necessary to see it as God Himself has unfolded it. God revealed Himself gradually. He began by calling Abraham. The Lord said to Abraham, "Go forth out of thy country, and from thy kindred, and out of thy father's house, and come into the land which I shall show thee. And I will make of thee a great nation, and I will bless thee, and magnify thy name, and thou shalt be blessed. I will bless them that bless thee, and curse them that curse thee, and in thee shall all the kindred of the earth be blessed" (Gen 12:1–4). God did not reveal His nature to Abraham. He told him only that He existed and that He was not aloof from man but rather was interested in man and his destiny. God made demands on Abraham, but He also gave a promise, a promise which was vague in Abraham's time but which would grow clearer and clearer with the passing of the centuries. God called Abraham, and Abraham had to respond to that call. In his response there was an element both of uncertainty and of certainty; Abraham had to leave the familiar surroundings of his father's house and his own country and go into the unknown, wherever God would lead him, but it was indeed God, clearly and unmistakably, Who spoke. What God required of Abraham by way of a response was a conversion—a turning away from himself, his own ways, his own plans, and a turning to God. Faith required of Abraham what it always requires of a man: a disintegration of his life and a reconstruction, a death to his old self and his old life which was centered on himself and a birth to a new life centered on God.

Moses, too, had to respond to God's call by a complete rearrangement of his life. He had to give up his simple, safe existence and embark on a new life as the leader of God's people. God rewarded Moses by entering into a deep and intimate relationship with him, and revealed Himself further. He showed that He controls history, that He is mightier than earthly kings and capable of compelling them to do His will.

Through Moses, God revealed Himself to the people of Israel. He reminded them of His care for them, His guidance, and His special love. He required of them in return that they reorient their lives to center on Him. They had to accept God as their only ruler and guide. God said to the Hebrews:

> I am the Lord thy god, who brought thee out of the land of Egypt, out of the house of bondage. Thou shalt not have strange gods before me. Thou shalt not make to thyself a graven thing, nor the likeness of anything that is in the heaven above, or in the earth beneath, nor of those things that are in the waters under the earth. Thou shalt not adore them, nor serve them: I am the Lord thy God, mighty, jealous, visiting the iniquity of the fathers upon the children, unto the third and fourth generation of them that hate me, and showing mercy unto thousands to them that love me, and keep my commandments. [Ex 20:1–7]

God required fidelity of the people, fidelity to Him like a wife's to her husband. When Israel sinned against faith by turning away from God and worshiping false gods, God Himself compared His people to an unfaithful wife: "Judge your mother, judge her, because she is not my wife, and I am not her husband. . . . For their mother hath committed fornication, she that conceived them is covered with shame, for she said: I will go after my lovers, that gave me my bread, and my water, my wool, and my flax, my oil, and my drink" (Os 2:4–7).

During the period of the judges God continued to care for His people. Time and again He had to punish them for their infidelity, but He came each time to their rescue when they finally turned to Him for help. Each time God answered by calling a man. He called Gedeon as he worked at his father's wine press. He called Samuel as he slept in his room in the Temple.

During the years of the kings God was with His people. He gave His Spirit to Saul as long as the king was worthy; He ruled through David; He gave His wisdom to Solomon. When the kingdoms began to decay, God sent His prophets to warn the people of the coming disaster. The hand of God was seen in the destruction. An earthly kingdom was not His goal. He revealed more and more about His Kingdom, an eternal kingdom, which was to await the coming of the great messianic king, the anointed of God—Christ.

In the midst of His people's sufferings during the period of exile in Babylon, God continued to reveal Himself to them. Speaking through His prophets, God told of His love and His mercy, and taught men more about His very being, His omnipotence, His omnipresence, His absolute perfection.

As God showed Himself each time, as He acted, as He brought about an encounter between Himself and a man or

His people, the man and the people responded. They turned from what they had been and had been doing and answered God's call. Gedeon left his father's fields and wine press and gathered together an army which would fight under God's banner and show His might. Samuel prepared himself for the vocation God gave him, that of judge and prophet. Saul, who later tried to do things his own way and was rejected, responded nonetheless for a time. David, despite his sins, became the greatest of the kings of Israel. The people to whom God spoke through the prophets during the Babylonian captivity responded with a revival of religious faith.

Through all the long centuries God revealed Himself more and more clearly to the world. He first called one man, then a people whom He bound to Himself by faith, and finally the whole world, to whom He revealed Himself through His Son Jesus Christ. God revealed Himself more completely in Christ, and accordingly expected and expects a greater response from man. Faith is to be firmly rooted in the person of Jesus Christ, the God-man. The Christian must accept Christ wholeheartedly, and must die to himself in order that Christ may live in him. Jesus expressed clearly the necessity for the disintegration and rebuilding of a man's life which faith demands: ". . . unless the grain of wheat falls into the ground and dies, it remains alone. But if it dies, it brings forth much fruit. He who loves his life, loses it; and he who hates his life in this world, keeps it unto life everlasting" (Jn 12:24–25).

To fail to see this great fact—that faith must go to the very roots of a man's life and rebuild it—is to fail to understand faith itself and consequently the meaning of the Christian life. The identification of faith with its intellectual aspect can easily give rise to a cold and rather business-like type of Catholicity. It can beget the kind of person who believes in the Trinity but never prays to the Trinity as such, because the Trinity seems to him to be associated with theology rather than with love and daily living. It can also produce a schizophrenic sort of Catholic, one whose belief is one thing and whose actions are another. He might answer a question about practical behavior by asking, "Do you want a regular answer or a religious answer?"

This kind of person has no difficulty accepting the Church's teaching as long as no problem arises to challenge the strength of his convictions. But when a challenge does arise he finds that standing between him and his goal is not a person, God, but a proposition, a truth to be adhered to. It is easy to say at such a time, "I know the Church teaches this, but I feel that God doesn't mind." This is the woman who has always "believed" the Church's teaching on divorce and remarriage; but when her drunken husband deserts her, leaving her with three young children, and a nice man comes along who wants to marry her, her attitude is, "Surely God does not expect me to waste my life in loneliness when I have a chance at happiness for myself and my children." Then there is the young couple who have no quarrel with the Church's doctrine on birth control when they come in to sign the papers before marriage, but who react to the doctor's advice to avoid pregnancy for a few years by saying, "The Church teaches that birth control is a sin, but God understands." And there is the person who has no trouble with the Church's teaching on justice and charity in racial matters until a Negro family wants to move into his block.

In all these instances, what was called faith was an intellectual acceptance of a truth or proposition. It was not an acceptance of a person, God, Who gave them this truth or proposition, as is evident from the readiness with which these people distinguish between the proposition and God when the chips are down.

The identification of faith with its intellectual aspect can give rise to another kind of Catholic—the "Sister said" or "I was told by a missionary priest" type. This is the person who accepts without question and as a matter of faith anything and everything said by anyone wearing a Roman collar or a wimple, whether the person speaking is giving the doctrine of the Church or not. This is the teen-ager who makes the rounds of confessors, hoping to find just one priest who will tell her that necking and petting are not mortal sins. This is the adult who clings to pious stories told him decades ago by a nun who was more conspicuous for her piety than her learning. This is the person who embarrasses his fellow Catholics and gives others a distorted idea of the Church by the outlandish statements he makes about the teachings of the Church. It may seem strange to claim that this sort of thing arises from an identification of faith with its intellectual content, and yet their error lies in the concept of faith as merely things to be believed.

At the other end of the spectrum is the Catholic who will believe only what can be shown to him to have been defined as an article of faith. Nothing less than a proposition *de fine definita* will do. Don't expect him to be impressed when you quote a papal encyclical. You might remind him that the Holy Father is speaking with the greatest authority, giving the teaching of Christ through His Church, but he will reply that the pope is not using his infallibility here, and therefore that what he says does not have to be accepted. For this man also, faith means giving intellectual assent—in his case, grudging and within as limited a scope as possible—to propositions. He does not see faith as a wholehearted acceptance of and dedication to a person.

If Catholics sometimes err by isolating the intellectual aspect of faith and identifying this one element with faith itself, there are others who err by going to the other extreme. These are the people who say, "It doesn't matter what you believe as long as you do your best and try to lead a good life." These people see faith as a commitment to God but they do not see it as a commitment of the whole person; they leave the intellect out. They agree that faith means a wholehearted acceptance of God, but fail to see it as an acceptance of God *as He is*. They do not acknowledge that faith must include a desire to know God as He is and to accept what He says.

This anti-intellectual approach is often that of people who wish to stress the fact that faith is superhuman. Actually, however, what they do is make faith inhuman. Instead of something supernatural and mysterious, which it is, they make it irrational and merely vague, and hence unnatural. Understood this way, faith can become simply a matter of the emotions, a sentimental penchant, a "feeling." This erroneous idea is at the heart of religious indifferentism, according to which all religions are equally good and pleasing to God. It ignores the fact that God has revealed Himself to man, or at least the fact that God intended man to understand that revelation and to take it seriously.

To believe in God, then, means to accept as true everything which God has revealed *and* to accept God Himself. Faith is an encounter with God. To believe in God means to respond to a personal God as a whole human person. True, the act of faith is an act of the intellect, but it is an act which is commanded by the will. Far from being an impersonal acceptance of a body of truth, faith is a surrender to God, a surrender not of the intellect alone but of the whole man. It is a falling in love with God. Love motivates belief. An act of faith is really in one sense an act of hope and an act of love as well.

The man who makes an act of faith is telling God that he accepts Him with his whole heart, puts all his trust in Him, and desires union with Him. The man who would say coldy, "I accept all that You have revealed as true, but I do not love You," would not be making an act of faith because he would be giving no honor to God. An act of faith gives great honor to God because it entails trust and love. St. James tells us that it is not enough merely to admit that God exists, that is, to accept revealed truth merely with the intellect, withholding one's heart from God. "The devils also believe," he says, "and tremble" (Jas 2:19).

Faith in God includes fidelity to God. The relation between God and the one who has faith in Him resembles the union of a man and woman in marriage. It is so described in Sacred Scripture; the prophets speak of Israel as Yahweh's bride, bound to God by the tie of faith, bound to be forever faithful to Him. When faith is understood in its full sense, the analogy between faith and the marital union can be clearly seen. Faith brings knowledge of God, not knowledge such as one would have of an algebraic equation but the knowledge which comes from the intimacy of love. Scripture speaks of marital relations as knowledge: "And Adam knew Eve his wife: who conceived and brought forth Cain . . ." (Gn 4:1). How perfect an expression that is! The true sexual union is the most perfect and complete union which can exist between two human beings. It involves a giving of the whole person and the acceptance of the whole person. It involves body and soul—heart, mind, feelings. It gives a knowledge of the other person such as no other union can give.

The knowledge of God which faith brings comes from a total union with God. This union is not attained merely by a use of the critical faculties; nor is it attained by a blind impulse, an animal feeling. A person can never be reached by either. A person can be reached only by the phenomenon of communion. Such is the case with faith. The encounter with God begins when God communicates with the human person, inviting him to unite himself to Him by faith. It is consummated when the human person throws himself open to the God Who calls him.

No marriage, no friendship, is quite the same as any other. These human relationships differ as the circumstances and the human beings involved differ. So it is with faith. Faith can be an incipient thing, or it can be deep and mature; one can know God in varying degrees. The man who has only a natural knowledge of God, who does not have supernatural faith, knows God only from the work of His hands. He sees the beautiful things that God has made and he knows that there is a God, but he has not heard the voice of God speaking to him in revelation. Another man may have real faith but only the minimum, the beginning of faith. He is like the prisoner in *The Count of*

Monte Cristo who knew that there was another prisoner in the next cell when he heard repeated tappings coming through the stone wall. Such a man knows that God has spoken—he accepts God—but he does not as yet know God well. Others know God as a man knows his friend. Still others advance to a deep intimacy with God which might be compared to that which a married couple achieve as their union deepens and mellows through the years.

"Now this is everlasting life," Jesus said, "that they may know thee, the only true God, and him whom thou hast sent, Jesus Christ" (Jn 17:3). The faith of a Christian is rooted in the person of Jesus Christ.

Jesus continually spoke of faith. He required it not only of His followers but even of anyone who sought a miracle. And by faith Christ meant the acceptance of Himself, not just the acceptance of what He said. Faith in Christ means the acceptance of Christ, Christ as He is—the whole Christ. Therefore, it means the acceptance of the Mystical Christ, the Body of Christ, the Church of Jesus Christ.

Christ did not cease to live and speak and act in the world when He ascended into Heaven; He lives on in His Church. He still reveals Himself through His Church, in the sense that the revelation given to the apostles is constantly developing and being clarified through the action of the Holy Spirit within the Church. The Catholic who says, "I know that the Church teaches this, but God understands," does not really have faith in Jesus Christ. He is like the man who accepts only the historical Christ, the Christ of the Gospels, the Christ Who walked the earth two thousand years ago. His faith does not embrace the whole Christ, Christ as He is today, living, teaching, and acting in His Church.

The man who says, "It doesn't matter what you believe as long as you do the best you can," is the same man who says, "I think that religion means living according to the golden rule." For this man, religion is primarily if not exclusively concerned with one's relationships with one's neighbors. Actually, this is not religion at all, since it leaves out the essence of religion—man's relationship to God. No Catholic who has had any instruction whatever would make this mistake. Catholics know that it makes a great deal of difference what one believes. They know that religion means above all one's relationship to God. Yet many Catholics, if asked what the worst sin is, would answer unhesitatingly murder or adultery, thus naming a sin which has to do with man's relationship with his neighbor.

In reality, the worst sins by far are those against faith. And the reason is that sins against faith strike at the most fundamental thing of all—one's relationship to God. It is faith which binds a man to God. Without faith it is impossible to have hope, it is impossible to have charity. "Without faith," says Holy Scripture, "it is impossible to please God" (Heb 11:6). The term which the Church uses to designate her own members is a very happy one: "the faithful." The faithful are those who are bound to God by the precious tie of faith. They are God's people. They belong to God. Their greatest mark of distinction is their faith, their fidelity to God. Even when they falter and fail, even when they fall into serious sin, God will forgive them and raise them up again. But when one of God's people becomes unfaithful—that is, sins against faith—he cuts himself off from God.

Good Catholics are convinced that the very worst thing that can happen to a man is for him to lose the faith. They are right in their conviction. There is always hope for a sinner who sins against love as long as he is still bound to God by faith. The man who sins against faith is much more apt to cut himself off from God completely and irrevocably. It seems strange to us today that society in the Middle Ages punished sins against faith by death, as we do the crime of murder. Yet, unacceptable as such a procedure would be today, it does bear witness to the horror in which sins against faith were held at that time. They were looked upon as the worst treason, treason against God Himself, a crime far greater than the crimes men committed through weakness or passion.

It is Himself God is offering when He offers the gift of faith. The gift is most precious, and one which must be prized above all others. But faith is not a gift like a wrist watch or a fur coat, something which adorns the person but which does not change. Faith is like the gift of life. It is meant to grow, to deepen, to develop, to mature. The unhappy fact is that many receive the gift of faith as the unprofitable servant received the talent from his master. The servant buried his talent in the ground instead of allowing it to increase. So it is with those who do not grow in knowledge of the faith.

It is sad to see a grown person saying prayers the same way he said them when he was a child. It is sad to find Catholic adults unable to explain what happens at Mass to anyone outside the Church who might ask for an explanation because they regard the Mass as a Sunday obligation, an event they are required merely to be present at or during which they are to pray privately rather than take an active part in. It is sad indeed to see Catholics—high-school and college graduates—consider the tremendous truths of the faith as some sort of routine facts to be believed but hardly wondered at and pondered over, and fail to see the Resurrection of Christ as the great event which gives meaning and joy to the Christian life.

All these are examples of Catholics whose faith has not matured because they did not deepen their knowledge of the faith. Often enough, these people are otherwise well educated and well informed, but they are religiously immature because they are content to live on the heritage of a grammar-school religious education. Sometimes an attempt to justify this failing is made on the grounds that further study might weaken one's faith. This was the attitude of one Catholic lady who was shocked when one of her friends asked the question, "Who made God?" The lady was reacting not to the absurdity of the question, as she might well have been, but to the fact that the questioner had the temerity to ask a question which had to do with religion. "You mustn't ask such a question," was her retort. "You must just believe." Of the two, the lady who asked the question was really the more reasonable. True, her question showed that she hadn't any idea at all of the meaning of divinity, but at least she was curious; she wanted to learn something about God. The other lady was quite unreasonable. She was horrified at the very idea of using reason in connection with the truths of the faith.

"Don't think about it—just believe" may appear at first to be an indication of a deep and unquestioning faith, which is commendable. More probably it is an indication of something else which is not commendable at all—sheer laziness. It could be a sort of religious inferiority complex, a conviction that a layman is not capable of knowing anything about his religion and should be content with believing, not reasoning about or looking further into what the priest tells him. Worst of all, it could be a faith so unsure of itself that it is afraid of examination.

The person who fears to learn more because he is afraid he might discover things he would find too hard to accept or might come at length not to a mystery but to an outright contradiction has a pretty shaky faith already. A childlike faith is a great thing; St. Thomas Aquinas had such a faith. But a childish faith is acceptable only in a child. As a man grows, his knowledge of the faith should grow. The more intelligent and learned a person is, the greater is his obligation to know his faith. And this is a matter of real obligation. An intelligent, literate Catholic adult should be abreast of Catholic doctrine. He should know the teachings of the popes. He should be well acquainted with serious Catholic writers. An intellectual who is a Catholic can hardly be excused for not studying St. Augustine and St. Thomas Aquinas, for example. Nowadays, when there is an abundance of really first-rate reading matter on Catholic doctrine, it is intolerable that there be an imbalance between secular knowledge and knowledge of the faith among Catholics.

In order for faith to grow and mature, its intellectual content must grow, but this growth is only part of the development which faith must undergo throughout a man's life. In fact, at each critical stage during life faith must change; the old faith must be re-formed into a new faith, one which is proper to the stage of development in which a man finds himself. Romano Guardini describes this process very well. Children, he says, perceive reality in a way peculiar to children:

> Work and play, symbol and object, fact and fancy are intermingled and make a world distinct from that of the grown-ups. The child's religion is of a like character. Divine and earthly reality, religious figures and the people about him, sacred teaching, legend and fairy tales all combine in a unity in which every part affects every other part. Criticism and revolt are still foreign to him. The struggles of thought and of life, in the true sense, have not yet begun.

Guardini says that the first crisis arises with the awakening of sex:

> The child no longer remains within the protective environment. He withdraws from it. Awareness of the infinite, boundless longings, vague hopes, measureless dreams stir within him. By this experience the maturing child is drawn away from parents and teachers. At the same time self-will and the rights of his own personality assert themselves. . . . The young person who is longing for the infinite has the feeling that his faith, still childish in form, has become too narrow. With his urge toward recognition, toward independence, toward action and the attainment of respect, he feels hampered by religious authority.

This is a crucial period, Guardini points out. If the crisis is weathered successfully, a new form of faith will follow—"the faith of the young person . . . an idealistic faith—fair, generous, luminous, but at the same time threatened on all sides with disillusionment."

In mature life, Guardini goes on to say, a new crisis develops. This occurs when the idealism and enthusiasm of youth begin to fade. At this stage the person faces stern reality. He is apt now to feel that the world of revelation is unreal and its demands fantastic. Once again there must be a reconstruction of the person's life, one which extends even to religious matters.

His faith must be freed from youthful idealism, and his whole way of thinking changed to one appropriate to his new stage of development, in which realism predominates. If he succeeds, the resulting faith will be that of the mature person; it will be a faith with stamina. This is a faith grounded not in enthusiasm and boundless expectation, but in steadfastness in the face of reality—a faith aware of difficulties and responsibilities, with a loyalty based not on emotions but on convictions and strength of mind.

But this is not the final form, Guardini says. As a person grows old and his memory records failure after failure, as he perceives his limitations, as his horizon narrows, there is disillusionment and a temptation to skepticism. Here, finally, there is need for a reconstruction. As a person enters into old age he engages in a struggle. If he comes through this struggle successfully he acquires wisdom, wisdom which can be acquired only after one has lived a long time and is near the end. His is the faith of old age.

Such faith is broad, understanding, tolerant. It is experience to the full—when it has humor in it. A wonderful thing, the humor of a religious man who carries everything into the boundless love of God, including the inadequate, the strange, the queer; who hopes for a solution when reason and effort can do no more, and who discerns a purpose where earnestness and zeal have long since given up hope of finding one.*

All too often, the development and reconstruction of faith to correspond with the critical developments in life which Guardini describes fail to happen. In this event, conflict arises, and in many cases faith withers away. An

*Quoted by John Heaney, S.J., (ed.) in *Faith, Reason and the Gospels* (Westminster, 1961), pp. 25–41.

adolescent, finding the faith of his childhood inadequate, may give up the faith. He realizes that his idea of God was very much like his image of Santa Claus. Instead of developing an adult idea of God, he decides that he does not believe in God. Something similar to this can occur at every crucial stage of life. If faith is not re-formed and does not grow and develop further, it may stagnate and disappear. A moral problem may arise, and one's faith may not be strong enough to stand up against it.

An habitual living in mortal sin may also slowly eat away at a man's faith as termites eat away at the supports of a house. Any real challenge may then be enough to cause the man to fall away from the Church. Sometimes not even a crisis is required; the man simply ceases to believe. Sin has done its work. Faith is closely bound up with the moral life. What a man does must be consistent with what he believes. It makes no sense for a married man to say, "I believe in the sanctity of marriage," and go on living with another woman. It is ridiculous for a man to say, "I believe that all men are sons of God and are to be treated as Christ would be treated," and in practice to treat others as things to be used and victimized in any way which benefits him financially or socially, without regard for their rights or their feelings.

The goal of faith is the interior transformation of a man according to the will of God. If this inner transformation does not take place, faith ceases to be a living thing. A man may go on believing, but his belief will be sterile and theoretical; it will have no influence on his life. He may try to justify himself by saying "*Credo* means 'I believe,' not 'I behave,'" but his attempt will be futile.

He may go on believing for a time, but unless he tries to live according to the precepts of his faith, he will eventually cease to believe. Faith and habitual mortal sin can coexist for a while, but as a rule one conquers the other in the long run. In some cases the façade may hold up; the man may continue to attend Mass, and he will not fall away from the Church. But there will be no interior life, no orientation of self to God, and often enough what such a man believes would be found upon examination to be rather different from what the Church teaches. He will have developed his own kind of faith, the only kind which is compatible with his way of life.

In some cases, when faith fails to develop with life, what happens is not a loss of faith but a descent into mediocrity. The result is a childish, immature faith, a faith which is inadequate to guide a mature person and make his a vigorous Christian life. Confession and Communion mean no more to this man now than they did when he was a child. Prayer remains at the level of the beginner. The person manifests not a deep liturgical piety but rather one which is devotion-centered. He may be attached to the Church and loyal to her, but he will fail really to understand and enter fully into her life.

In order for faith to grow and develop as a person grows and develops through life, it is necessary for him to understand that the truths of faith can be expressed in different ways. He must understand that while God doesn't change He expresses Himself differently to different people at different times, that while truth remains the same it is expressed differently according to the needs of the learner. A small child, with his vivid imagination and love of the wonderful, accepts literally the story of creation in six days with ease. His imagination delights in the picture of God forming man's body with His hands out of clay, as a potter forms a vase. Only by hearing things in this way will a child be able to understand the truth which Scripture conveys.

An adult Catholic should know that he is not expected to stop his ears to the words of perfectly sane scientists and cling to a literal and fundamentalist interpretation of accounts like this in Scripture. He should know in this instance that all the Bible is teaching is that God made the world, not that He made it in six days or in six periods of time, and that God made man. He should realize that the six days are simply a literary devise, used to make it easier to remember the story and to provide an explanation to the Hebrews of the Law of God which ordered them to rest on the seventh day of each week. The Bible is not a book of science, and it does not have a word to say about whether man's body evolved from a lower species or not, being content to teach the important religious truth—that man was made by God, a fact which is true whether God made man by a direct act or by a process of evolution which He directed. Grown people are sometimes shocked when they discover what Scripture studies bring to light about the message of the Bible. One sometimes hears the anguished cry, "These people are destroying my faith!" Actually, what is being destroyed is the childish form in which faith was presented to the child. What should emerge is a more adult faith, a better, more mature understanding of God and of the message of salvation He has given us.

Faith also expresses itself differently according to time,

place, and temperament. Some people outside the Church bemoan the fact that Catholics everywhere believe the same thing. From this they conclude that there is a dull sameness about Catholics the world over. Actually, such is not the case at all. American Catholics are just as amazed (and sometimes shocked) as their Protestant compatriots when they observe Italian Catholics in Rome shouting at the tops of their lungs right in church as the pope enters St. Peter's. American, English, and Irish Catholics are sometimes disturbed by the casual attitude which they consider Latin Catholics have toward the laws of the Church. A group of American priests, traveling by train in Italy on a Friday, were outraged when they found no meatless dishes on the menu in the diner. They were puzzled at the amused looks on the faces of the other passengers, presumably Catholics, and all happily eating spaghetti with meat sauce, when they indignantly ordered the spaghetti without any sauce. What they did not know was that the law of abstinence is interpreted in a different way in Italy. You are regarded as excused when you are traveling. On the other hand, Latin Catholics might be dissatisfied with what seems to them like a coldness and legalism in our expression of faith. One old Italian woman was astonished at being shushed when she laughed out loud in church. As she said, "Why should not a member of the family laugh in her Father's house?"

As any world traveler can testify, Catholics in each country are different, even though they profess the same faith. All one need do is compare the Latin and Eastern rites to see how differently the same faith can be expressed. The language is different, the ceremonies of the Mass are differ-

V.G.

ent. The words of consecration, whispered in the Latin rite, are sung in some of the Eastern rites. Eastern rite Catholics do not genuflect; they have another, very impressive gesture of adoration. They do not use holy water as Western rite Catholics do. They have icons instead of statues in their churches. They follow a different liturgical calendar from that of Latin rite Catholics.

Far from compelling uniformity in these matters, the Church is very eager to preserve the different rites. She is also careful to preserve the customs and practices of people in missionary countries. The one true faith must be given to all men, the Church realizes, but it must be given to each people in a form which fits its culture, a form it can understand. A priest in any Western country wears white vestments on Easter and, of course, keeps his shoes on in the sanctuary. Such actions would be quite out of place in Japan, where white is considered to be a color of mourning and shoes are never worn inside the house. Gregorian chant sounds perfectly fine in a Benedictine monastery in France; it would sound a bit strange in a thatched-roof hut which serves for a church in Central Africa.

Care must always be taken not to identify faith itself with forms and practices which are connected with it. These can and should change as conditions change. The faith itself is unchangeable. Some people become so accustomed to familar forms and practices that they are shocked and even scandalized when they see them give way to different ones. They say, "What is happening to the Church? They've changed everything around in Holy Week. They've changed the fast before Communion. They tell me there is no St. Philomena. I don't know what to believe any more!" People who are bewildered by changes like these should remind themselves that the Church has always changed forms and practices in order to make the manner of presenting the faith more effective. The Church changed the language of the liturgy from the original Aramaic in which Christ offered the first Mass. The Western Church changed from Greek into Latin when conditions warranted it, and adopted the practice of distributing Holy Communion under the appearance of bread alone. Throughout the centuries, she has continued to renew and re-form herself, changing whatever needed to be changed, and she will continue to do so. But it must be remembered that what changes is not the faith itself but only the manner in which it is expressed and professed.

Faith, as everyone knows, is a free gift from God. It is a mystery known only to God why He offers faith in different ways to different people. The ordinary way in which God gives faith is in the sacrament of Baptism. Again, it is a mystery why some receive faith through Baptism in infancy while others receive it only later in life. We use the word *convert* for those who come into the Church as adults. Yet even those who have received faith through Baptism as infants must, in a sense, be converted in later life. Everyone must have an encounter with God before he really undergoes the orientation to God which faith demands, that disintegration and rebuilding of one's life which is the response to faith. The faith is there all the time; it has been given in Baptism. The response to faith which initiates its growth and its development into maturity is what must come later. This, too, must be prompted by God.

It is God Who brings about the encounter which calls for man's response. Sometimes this encounter takes place dramatically, even miraculously, as it did in the case of St. Paul on the road to Damascus and St. Francis of Assisi in the chapel of St. Mary of the Angels. Sometimes it comes in the form of a crisis in one's life—the death of a loved one, a serious illness, an accident, a narrow escape from injury or death. Sometimes it comes from something which is read, as it did with St. Ignatius Loyola. Sometimes it comes from something which was said in a sermon or in the advice of a confessor. In most cases this encounter with God comes about almost unperceived, as God gently draws the soul to a gradual realization of his relationship to Him by a long series of interior graces. All the person knows is that he now realizes more clearly that his life should be centered on God.

Every convert has had a different history. Each has found faith in a different way. In the case of "cradle Catholics," too, God deals in His own way with each individual. In every case there must be a conversion—in fact, a whole lifetime of conversions—if faith is to grow to maturity. This rebuilding of faith must go on and on, as Guardini points out. It is a gradual process, and an uneven one. There will be setbacks. The human being will falter; he may even fail at times. There may be sin and lack of fidelity to God. But there will be also repentance and the renewal of faith which it entails. If the man whom God has called and blessed with the gift of faith perseveres and grows in the faith, the Holy Spirit will bring him to maturity as a Christian and form Christ in him.

4

Prayer: Man's Approach to God

At a convention of high-school students who were interested in the lay apostolate, a meeting was taking place on ways and means of applying Christian principles to student life. One of the girls asked for the floor and suggested that the delegates pray for God's help and guidance. At that, a boy jumped to his feet and shouted, "We don't want prayer, we want Catholic action!" To the credit of the assembly, this remark was greeted with gales of laughter. The crowd knew something that the young enthusiast forgot—that prayer is a matter of the utmost importance.

If faith calls for a response from man, as has been said, the first and most immediate form which that response must take is prayer—the worship of God. A man's first response to beauty is to go out to the object in some way, to give his praise to it, often physically by a gasp, a gesture, a change in facial expression. A man responds to truth by a nod of the head. He responds to kindness by feeling gratitude; he says "Thank you" when someone gives him something or does him a favor. Man's first response to God, like other responses, is a natural and immediate one: he praises God, he worships God, he prays. The very thought of God includes some idea of His supreme excellence and man's total dependence on Him. The response of worship is an acknowledgment of that excellence and dependence.

The response of prayer which man gives to God is a matter of obligation. The first commandment binds all men under sin to pray at certain times during their lives. The Church helps us fulfill that obligation by binding us under sin to offer Mass on Sundays and holy days of obligation. It is hardly necessary to point out that anyone whose prayer life is limited to the minimum to which he is obliged under sin would be religiously immature in the extreme. The religiously mature person prays not only often but also well. His prayer is an expression of his faith and his love, which are a mature faith and a mature love.

A person who is religiously mature realizes that while he praises God and gives glory to Him by his prayers, it is not for God's sake that he prays. He knows that God does not need his praise and adoration, that it is he himself who needs prayer, that only through prayer will he learn to know God and deepen his intimacy with God. He knows that only through prayer will he come to a fuller appreciation of the tremendous facts of the faith and increase in love and develop spiritually as God intends him to.

Prayer, then, corresponds to a deep human need. One would therefore expect it to be an easy and a common thing; the worship of God should be acknowledged by all to be the most important thing a man does. Not much observation is needed to show that such is not the case. How many people pray at all? How many pray only in times of danger? How many pray in the sense of offering praise and worship to God instead of merely asking for favors?

A scene comes to mind. It is a warm, pleasant Sunday morning in a poor section of a large city, the kind of neighborhood where people live outdoors as much as possible during the summer. The church has filled and emptied five times already this morning for the earlier Masses. Now it is time for the last Mass. People are coming from four directions and entering the church. These are the people of the neighborhood—some of them. The majority? Hardly. It is a very crowded section, and most of the people are supposed to be Catholics. Even if they were hanging from the rafters at all the Masses, the church would never be able to hold all the Catholics if they all came to Mass. Where are the others? One can see them by merely letting one's gaze sweep along the street. They are out with buckets and hoses, washing their cars. They are loading their automobiles with picnic hampers and bathing suits for a trip to the park or the beach. They are sitting on their front porches in T shirts and house dresses, idly observing, without the slightest feeling of guilt or shame, the people who are on their way to church. They have not been to an earlier Mass; they never go.

And what of the large numbers of non-Catholics living in the neighborhood, those who, if asked their religion, might reply "Baptist" or "Presbyterian," but who really have no church affiliation whatever and never go to any church? Do these people pray at all? Do they ever think of worshiping God? One could hardly say with any assurance that they do. It could be argued that it is not fair to conclude that people do not pray just because they don't go to church on Sunday, but the conclusion would seem to be justified. A Catholic who never goes to Mass on Sunday can be presumed to have a prayer life which verges on the nonexistent, and people not affiliated with any church usually have so little knowledge of God that they wouldn't know how to go about praying to Him if they thought of doing so in the first place.

What, then, of the assertion that the worship of God should be natural and instinctive to man? It is still true, philosophically. According to his nature, man should be aware of God and conscious of the necessity of worshiping Him. But in the dehumanized atmosphere of the post-religious world in which we live today, man does not act naturally. In the asphalt jungle the things which seem real are the automobile, the television set, and the filter-tipped cigarette, not the spiritual world, not an unseen God. It has been said that modern man is like a wolf, roaming the wasteland that is Western civilization, howling his hunger for God. But he doesn't know his hunger is for God, and his howls take the form of singing rock-and-roll ballads and drinking beer in a room illuminated only by the eerie light of the television or, if he can afford it, pursuing *la dolce vita*. If modern man does not pray, does not worship God, it is because he is not aware of God. This in itself is a monstrous state of affairs.

Such is people's ignorance of prayer and its relation to man's nature that there are those who regard prayer as beneath human dignity, as cowardly. This attitude would be logical for an atheist, who would think a man a fool to bow down before nothing and address words to someone who doesn't exist. But for anyone who admits the existence of a personal God, this attitude is absurd. No one would regard a man who refuses to say "Thank you" as more a man because of it; everyone would see him for the selfish, ungrateful boor that he is. No one would consider a man who refuses to pay his debts or to recognize his obligations more a man for this, either; quite to the contrary. The old Hebrew proverb says it very well: "He who eats and drinks and does not praise God is a thief."

Among the many beautiful and touching scenes in Marc Connelly's play *The Green Pastures* is one in which the Lord pays a visit to the earth to see how mankind is getting along. God is appalled as He comes upon one group after another. He sees a drunken couple staggering along the road; He sees an indecently dressed woman parading shamelessly before a group of leering men; He comes upon some men shooting craps—and all this on the Lord's Day. God is cut to the heart. "Have they forgotten all about Me?" He asks Himself. "Don't they care at all?" Just then the Lord passes a bush in full flower. As God approaches, the flowers light up, and in a chorus of children's voices they shout, "Good morning, Lord." God's face breaks out in a wonderful smile. Some of His creatures, at least, appreciate His goodness to them and are happy to greet Him.

One gets the feeling that the animals and flowers would praise God consciously in words if they could; they are so faithful to their natures, obedient to the laws which God has given them. But the only way nature can praise God is the way it does praise Him—by showing forth His goodness and beauty. Man alone can know the goodness of God. Man alone can respond to God. Man alone can praise God in the strict sense of the word. And the fact that man has the power of knowing and praising God is, naturally speaking, his greatest glory. Man is an animal, and he has many things in common with them—he eats, he sleeps, he mates and reproduces. But unlike the brutes, man prays. There is nothing even analogous to prayer among the animals. A man is never more truly himself, never farther removed from the brutes, than when he prays, for in praying he uses his highest faculties for the highest purpose in the most perfect and exalted way.

In prayer, as in everything else, Christ is the perfect example. In Christ God shows us the perfect man, manhood at its very best, and Christ is above all a man of prayer. Prayer was the very life of Jesus. There was not a moment when He was not in communion with His Father. His every action was a prayer, an act of adoration of God. He prayed before every important action. Time and again the Gospels tell us that as Jesus was about to perform a cure He would raise His eyes to Heaven and speak to His Father. How often, too, do the Gospels show Jesus going off by Himself to pray, sometimes throughout the whole night. It must have been an unforgettable sight to see Christ at prayer. No wonder the apostles pleaded with Jesus to teach them to pray as He did.

Prayer might be described simply as contact with God. It is not merely thinking about God, although thinking about God can be a prelude to prayer. Prayer is communication with God, conversation with God. This communication can be in words, expressed either with the lips or entirely in the mind and heart. It can also be a wordless communication, like that between lovers, who express their love by their delight at simply being in each other's presence. This is the kind of prayer which was practiced by an old man who used to sit in the back of the church for hours at a time in the little town of Ars in France. The holy Curé had long observed the old man. One day he saw that the man was smoking his pipe in church, and decided he should speak to him. After gently informing him that it was not proper to smoke in church, the Curé asked the old man, "What do you do all the time as you sit here in the rear of the church?" Gesturing toward the tabernacle, the old man replied, "I just look at Him, and He looks at me, and we love one another."

An action, too, can be a prayer if it is a conscious and loving performance of God's will, something done for the glory of God. Such an action is prayerful because it is an act of adoration, an act of worship, a loving submission of oneself to God, a giving of oneself to God. This is the essential element in prayer—this giving of oneself to God. A formal prayer, a prayer of words, even if it be a prayer of petition, is such a giving of oneself. When a man prays, he gives God his acknowledgment of need, his belief in God's power to help, his confidence that God will answer his prayer. In a worshipful action a man gives God himself by giving his energy, his attention, everything which goes into the performance of the act. Christ's life was a life of prayer, a life of worship. It was a continual giving of Himself to the Father. The culmination of Christ's life was the supreme act of worship He offered when He gave His life to God by dying on the cross.

Christ's prayer won the admiration of the apostles. They had watched, unmoved, many times as the Pharisees intoned their long prayers in public. The big words, the studied gestures, the stentorian tones failed to impress them. The apostles had often observed the priests also as they performed their sacred duties. These, too, were supposed to be prayer, and yet they were done so perfunctorily, so mechanically, so hastily and thoughtlessly. Jesus' prayer was different. When Christ prayed He was absorbed in God. He gave Himself over completely to something He obviously considered to be of the greatest importance. There were no empty words here, no hastily muttered phrases. This was prayer which came from the heart. This was communion with God.

One might expect that with the example of true prayer which Christ gave and with His insistence on complete sincerity in prayer, His followers would be free from the faults which marred the prayers of the Pharisees and the Jewish priests. Yet as far as Catholics are concerned the record does not show that such is the case. Catholics may pray more than other people do, but by and large how well do Catholics pray?

A Catholic woman and her Protestant friend were present at a wake when the priest came in to say the usual five Our Fathers and Hail Marys. The Protestant woman knelt down with the others but did not answer the prayers. Afterwards, the Catholic woman asked her why. She replied that she did not know the prayers the priest had said. "Why, surely you know the Lord's Prayer!" her friend exclaimed. "Was that the Lord's Prayer?" the Protestant woman asked in genuine astonishment. "I didn't recognize it." Then she turned the knife in the wound by adding, "When we say the Lord's Prayer we say it slowly and reverently."

It would be nice if there were no truth in the accusation that Catholics rush through their prayers without paying much attention to what they are saying, but our own ears tell us otherwise when we pause to listen. Often this faulty way of praying begins in early childhood and persists throughout adult life. Any priest can testify that some of the things children say in the Act of Contrition are pure nonsense—"I fear the laws of Heaven" or "the lost of Heaven," "Most of all because I defend Thee, my God, Who aren't all good," or "Who are tall, good and deserving of all my sins." The possibilities seem to be endless, just in this one prayer. Of course, these are children; one does not expect them to pray like adults. The trouble is that all too often when the children grow up they continue to pray like children. They correct the mistakes in the Act of Contrition, but sometimes they go on praying carelessly, saying words very rapidly and thoughtlessly, as if the words themselves were effective, no matter how they are said. This is a sort of occupational disease to which Catholics are especially prone. They learn so many prayer formulas and use them so often that, as we have said, they can come to assume that it is the formula itself rather than the raising of the mind and heart to God in using the formula which constitutes prayer.

There is nothing wrong with a prayer formula, of course; far from it. The most perfect of all prayers—the Lord's Prayer—is a formula. Prayer formulas, or vocal prayers as they are called, are extremely useful. The Church gives them to us in order to help us pray, to enable us to say what we should say to God. The Act of Contrition, for example, expresses everything which a sinner needs to tell God when he seeks God's pardon. Almost every word in this prayer is necessary for this purpose. The Church provides formulas for every kind of prayer. In her liturgy she uses set forms of prayer, words which have been part of her worship for ages, including the inspired songs from Holy Scripture, the psalms. The Church intends these formulas, these vocal prayers, to be said with the mind and heart, not merely with the lips. The trouble arises when the words which are meant to express the sentiments of the one who is saying them are said thoughtlessly.

Protestants are less inclined toward this kind of thoughtless vocal prayer. Protestantism itself stresses the efforts of the individual in the first place; a Protestant is less likely to "coast with the Church" and therefore more apt to put more of himself in his prayers. He has to rely more on his own imagination because he is much more on his own; he has to pray in his own words because he doesn't have at his disposal the many formulas which the Catholic has. This can be less than a blessing, of course. The story is told of a dying soldier who wanted desperately to pray and could find no words but "Now I lay me down to sleep." On the other hand, too great a reliance on prayer formulas can have the effect of stunting the growth of one's prayer life. Christian maturity requires more than vocal prayer; it requires some sort of mental prayer.

It is not easy to give a good answer to a question which Protestants sometimes ask: "Why do you say the Lord's Prayer five times? Why don't you say it once very slowly and thoughtfully instead?" Certainly, this practice is common among Catholics. It is even sometimes official; we are asked to say so many Our Fathers and Hail Marys for the intention of the Holy Father. The usual penance given in confession is a number of Our Fathers and Hail Marys. So ingrained is this practice that it is difficult to depart from it even when a real effort is made. One priest tried to give more meaningful penances in confession, with the following result:

PRIEST: Now, for your penance, spend three minutes telling our Lord in your own words that you love Him and will try to imitate Him during the next week.
PENITENT: Yes, Father—and what is my penance?
PRIEST: As I said, spend three minute talking to our Lord.
PENITENT: And my penance?
PRIEST: That is your penance.
PENITENT: But what shall I say for my penance?
PRIEST (defeated): Five Our Fathers and five Hail Marys.
PENITENT: Thank you, Father.

The expression *mental prayer* frightens some people. They associate it with St. John of the Cross or St. Theresa, great mystics who scaled the heights of prayer. But this association is not necessary. A great virtuoso like Horowitz or Rubinstein plays the piano; so does the fellow who hammers out "Chopsticks." St. John of the Cross used mental prayer; so does anyone who converses with God in his own words. The trouble is that in the past not enough was expected of the laity. Mental prayer or meditation was regarded as something for the monastery, the seminary, or the convent. The layman simply was not up to it; let him be content with his repeated Our Fathers and Hail Marys it was thought.

Nowadays, more and more lay people are coming to see that mental prayer is necessary for anyone who wishes to advance in the spiritual life. They realize, too, that it is not such a difficult thing as the term seems to imply. Anyone can pray mentally simply by thinking of the words of a vocal prayer, such as the Our Father, and pausing after a phrase to allow the words to sink in. Instead of saying the usual five Our Fathers, one merely thinks over the expression "Our Father" for a moment. It then becomes easy and natural to feel gratitude to God for all that He is and does and to express that gratitude and love in one's own words or thoughts. One can pray mentally by using a book as a starting point, also. The Scriptures are, of course, excellent for this purpose, but *The Imitation of Christ* or any spiritual book will prove fruitful. One merely reads a sentence or a paragraph and then pauses to reflect on it. Some thought will occur every once in a while which it will be natural to express to God.

It is easy to turn other things into mental prayer, too—the examination of conscience before confession, for example. Often enough this is merely an impersonal exercise in soul-searching, but it could be a conversation with God, an examination of one's conscience with God's help. Instead of "Let's see—did I lose my temper this week?" one could pray, "Lord, help me see how often I offended You by losing my temper this week." The Stations of the Cross can be made very easily without a book simply by reflecting on the scene at each station for a moment and expressing to God the thoughts which come into the mind. The same procedure can be used with morning and evening prayers and with the thanksgiving after Holy Communion.

Breaking away now and then from the same familiar—even overfamiliar—words and sentences will have the effect of fostering a more personal effort. One who becomes used to talking to God in his own words in this way will find it easier to fit longer periods of real mental prayer into his day.

Some people are deterred from achieving maturity in prayer by a false impression. They associate private prayer with sentimentality and bad taste. They are repelled by pictures and statues which are artistically atrocious and which seem to invite one not so much to pray as to indulge in a sort of orgy of religious emotion. They have read and heard prayers which seem to them extravagant and sentimental. They don't feel the emotions which the words of these prayers describe. It seems wrong to them to say that their hearts overflow with rapture every time they hear the word *Jesus* or *Mary* when they and God know perfectly well that this is not true. Instead of learning to pray realistically and sincerely by learning to meditate or by discovering the many good, solid vocal prayers contained in the liturgy, these people often conclude that they are just not pious or not the praying type. They content themselves with passive presence at Mass, routine reception of the sacraments, and perhaps a hasty, brief, and formalized morning and evening prayer.

There is another group of people who fail to achieve maturity in prayer because of this sentimentality in religious art and devotions. These are the people who like it or think they like it but who really accept it because they don't know anything else. These are good people, people who want to pray more, who want to do more than the minimum. They come to services, no matter what the service, because they are eager to take part in the Church's prayer life. There is a well-known type, of course, the person who thrives on sentimentality and who is overpious in a rather unhealthy sense, and he—or more frequently she—is also to be found at every service held in church. But the majority of people who come to private devotions are not of this type. They would respond to something better.

This fact was demonstrated by the experience of one priest who, at the request of a diocesan organization, substituted a Bible vigil for the usual weekly perpetual novena service. The vigil service consisted of the singing of psalms, the reading of several passages from Holy Scripture, homilies given by the priest, and prayers taken from the missal. The pastor was not without misgivings, anticipating some sort of outcry from the "regulars," who were in the old familiar rut with their novena prayers. Quite unexpectedly, there was no protest at all; on the contrary, many of the people who had been reciting the other prayers week after week with seeming contentment expressed their delight at the change and asked whether such a service might not be held regularly.

These remarks are not meant to belittle novenas or any other form of devotion approved by the Church, but simply to emphasize the fact that the Church encourages private devotions as an outlet for the piety of people of different tastes and temperaments. She warmly approves them, since they can deepen the spiritual life of the faithful and prepare them to take part in the liturgy—the official and public prayer of the Church—more fruitfully. It is to be expected that the prayers which are part of these private devotions will be less restrained than those found in the liturgy. The prayers of the liturgy are for all; they are the prayers of the whole family of God. Private prayers are for the individual. They often express more personal feeling than do liturgical prayers. Good private prayer can be expressive of feelings without being sentimental. What is objectionable is the kind of prayer which expresses a false piety, which is based on emotion and sentimentality rather than on solid love and faith and goes counter to the idea of the Mystical Body.

Offensive, too, are prayers which express theologically inaccurate ideas or which make the wrong emphasis—an act of contrition, for example, in which the sole motive for sorrow for sin is that the sinner has "wounded the heart" of our Blessed Mother (nothing about having offended God is said), or a prayer which equates the objective, infinite sacrifice which Christ offered on the cross with a metaphorical sacrifice which was "offered on the heart of Mary." Prayers which are as theologically offcenter as this are not likely to promote a solid and mature prayer life.

Some people are prevented from maturing in their prayer life by outright superstition, which they actually mistake for genuine faith and piety. Catholics know that carrying a rabbit's foot for good luck or refusing to sit thirteen at a table is downright wrong conduct. Superstition among Catholics is apt to take a different form—so many Masses must be said on consecutive days or they won't have their effect. Or this prayer must be recited at three o'clock every afternoon for ten days; if you say it that way you will obtain from St. Remigius what you pray for, no matter how difficult it may be, but if you miss a day you will have bad luck. "Father, today would be the last day of my novena, and the doctor says I must stay in bed. Will I have to start all over again?" The mechanical repetition of the words of a prayer smacks of superstition, too. It is not too unlike the Buddhist prayer wheel. In both cases there is the assumption that words, whether written or spoken, can be effective as a prayer all by themselves, without the involvement of mind and heart.

The Ash Wednesday Catholic and the Palm Sunday

Catholic are a breed apart. They are not good Catholics who have been sidetracked and have failed to achieve religious maturity. The Ash Wednesday Catholic comes to Church just exactly once a year—on Ash Wednesday, to "get ashes." His motive is obscure, no doubt even to himself. A psychologist might discover why—perhaps this person regards ashes as a pledge of eternal life or at least as a guarantee of good luck. (The Palm Sunday—or Second Passion Sunday—Catholic is, of course, the Ash Wednesday Catholic, *mutatis mutandis.*) These characters are religious freaks. They need not concern us here. But good Catholics often seem to display an attitude toward sacramentals which is reminiscent of the Ash Wednesday Catholic's. They must regard ashes as somehow efficacious in themselves rather than merely as a sign of an intention to do penance during Lent. Why else would they bring babies up to receive ashes?

Religious immaturity shows itself again and again in the way people use the sacramentals, though not many are like the man who asked the priest for a medal for his sick baby to swallow. He scoffed at the idea of pinning a medal on the baby, saying, "How can you cure something on the inside by pinning something on the outside?" But there are those who seem to prefer the sacramentals to the sacraments. On Good Friday everyone comes up to venerate the cross, while only about half the congregation come up to receive Communion.

Superstition shows itself, too, in the use some people make of vigil lights. Vigil lights are not sacramentals. One wonders sometimes what on earth some people think they are. In one downtown church in a large city, people stand in line waiting to light vigil lights. And they light them, mind you, not with a taper but automatically, by inserting a dime in a slot; for these are electric vigil lights, modern, efficient, clean, and bearing an unfortunate resemblance to a pinball machine. The vigil light, whether electric or waxen, can be a trap for some people. There are those who come to the altar rail not for Communion but only after Mass, to pray before a statue and light a vigil light. Some give the impression that they regard vigil lights as more efficacious than prayer. Their first thought when they seek a special favor from God is not to pray, not to offer Mass, but to light a candle.

A mature prayer life is centered on the two most precious gifts which God has given to man: the Eucharist and the word of God. It is liturgical, that is, it finds its expression in and takes its inspiration from the official and public prayers of the Mystical Body, the liturgy. As we have said, the mature Catholic does not disregard private prayer and devotions, of course; on the contrary, he is well aware of what the Church teaches—that these are vital and utterly necessary. Private prayer, especially in the form of meditation and devotions to our Lady and to the saints, and spiritual reading are indispensable in the prayer life of a Catholic. The mark of maturity in the use of these means is that it centers about the core and heart of Christian worship, the liturgy—the Mass, the sacraments, the sacramentals, and the divine office. The Catholic whose prayer life is truly mature says the rosary, but he doesn't say it during Mass, when the whole congregation is praying and singing together as the Church asks us to. The rugged individualist who refuses to take an active part in the Mass does not understand the Mass as group worship, a family act. His piety is not truly Catholic.

One young man, a very pious person, explained to a priest why he did not join in the prayers of the congregation at Mass. He was praying for a deceased friend, and wanted to gain as many indulgences for him as possible. He reasoned that if he said the rosary during Mass he would gain a plenary indulgence, which would be more valuable than what he would gain by participating in the Mass. This young man was well-intentioned, but he was in error about the meaning of the Mass. His piety was sincere, but immature and offcenter because it was not liturgical. In the first place, the young man failed to realize that the Mass is, above all, an act of worship of God. Primarily, it is an offering made to God. We ask for gifts from God in the Mass, we pray for ourselves and others, we may offer Mass for a specific person, but the fact remains that we go to Mass primarily not to get something but to give something. The young man was thinking only of what he could get from God. He should have been thinking, first of all, of giving himself completely—his mind, his voice, his own inclinations and preference for privacy—in the interests of the great family act of worship of God. And incidentally, who could doubt that he would gain far more for his deceased friend by entering fully into the Mass, whether or not he called it a plenary indulgence?

We said earlier that the mature Christian is free—free from the preoccupation with laws which plagues the legalist. This freedom is to be found in the realm of prayer, too. The mature Christian prays not because he has to but because he wants to. Moral theologians tell us that we have an obligation under sin to pray at certain times—in time of temptation when we would otherwise succumb, and "from time to time" during our life. The legalist often considers himself bound under pain of sin to say morning and evening prayers and grace at meals, and confesses his failure to say these prayers when he goes to confession. The mature Catholic knows that he is not bound under sin to pray at these times, but he does pray at these times. He prays upon rising simply because he wants to greet God first thing in the morning and offer his day to Him. He prays before retiring because he wants to ask God's pardon for his shortcomings during the day and to thank God for the blessings he has received. When he oversleeps and has no time to say morning prayers on his knees, the mature Catholic does not regard the omission as something which has to be told in confession. The mature Christian doesn't worry about his obligation to pray any more than a man who truly loves his wife worries about his obligation to love her. He is not concerned with the minimum which he must give to God by way of prayer. His intimacy with God is such that his mind and heart turn to God, if only for a second, again and again throughout the day. Prayer, for him, is not unusual and unnatural; it is simply a part of his life, something which flows naturally from his faith and his love.

This is not to say that the mature Catholic always finds it easy to pray. Even the saints had periods of spiritual dryness during which prayer was very difficult. A person who prays only when he "feels religious" and thinks that a prayer said without any such feeling is not a good prayer is quite immature spiritually. A small child does what he feels like doing; a mature person does what he knows he should do. He even wants to do what love requires, although his feelings might not agree. It is the same with prayer. A mature Catholic is mature in his faith. Therefore, he is mature in that response to faith which is prayer.

5

Seven Signs of God's Love

It was just as the priests were sitting down to dinner that the telephone rang. "Father, can you come over right away? Grandma seems to be dying."

The priest put down the receiver, ran upstairs to his room for his oil stock, ritual, and stole, dashed over to the Church to get the Blessed Sacrament, and was off. In a few minutes he was ringing one of the bells in the vestibule of a large apartment building. A buzzer sounded. The priest opened the inner door and climbed the stairs to the third floor. A teen-age girl with curlers in her hair was waiting at the open door of the apartment. She was not holding a candle. Her manner could best be described as friendly, in an offhand sort of way. "Hi, Father," she said. Then, pointing down the hall, she added, "Grandma's in the last room to the left."

The priest entered the apartment, almost colliding with a man who was making his way into the front room with a can of beer and a newspaper. As he passed the kitchen, he caught a glimpse of a man and woman seated at a table, smoking. The dying woman lay in the back room, quite alone. There on a table next to the bed was the linen cloth, the crucifix, the lighted candles, the cotton, and the water and spoon. The priest heard the old lady's confession, anointed her, and gave her Viaticum. She would live for maybe a few days longer, the priest judged; no need yet for the prayers for the dying. He gave the old lady a final blessing and turned to make his way once more down the hall.

The man and woman who had been in the kitchen were waiting for him now at the front door. The man with the can of beer was reclining on a sofa, wholly absorbed in his newspaper. The couple at the door, however, were friendly —even grateful. The woman flashed a bright smile and said, "Thank you so much for coming, Father. I am so glad that Mother was able to get the last sacraments."

Mother got the last sacraments—that summed up the situation. Something was done for Mother, something good and holy and highly desirable. But in the minds of the members of this family, it was a ritual which concerned only the sick person; it was something the Church did for her. There was no thought that this ritual was an act of worship in which the whole Church was involved, in which they themselves were involved and should have taken part.

How different it was in the case of another dying woman. This lady, upon hearing that she had only a month to live, asked if she might be anointed in the parish church after Mass on Sunday with her friends and neighbors, her fellow parishioners, present to take part in the ritual. At first the pastor thought this an odd request. On second thought he decided that it made sense. A member of Christ's Body was being prepared by Christ Himself for entrance into Heaven. This was, after all, something which concerned the whole Christian community. How fitting that the people of the parish should be present and take part.

Admittedly, a public anointing is rare and unusual. But the attitude which prompted the woman to ask for it and the pastor to agree to it is quite correct, in sharp contradistinction to the attitude of the family of the other dying woman. They erroneously regarded the sacrament as a purely private matter and as something which one only receives. They failed to recognize this and all the sacraments for what they are—part of the worship of the Church.

In a sense there is only one sacrament: Christ, the God-man. Christ is the very embodiment of the idea of sacrament, which is an inner, invisible reality which is manifested by an external sign. Christ is the greatest of realities, God Himself, the invisible God, appearing, living, and acting through a visible human nature. And it is Christ Himself who acts in and through the seven sacraments. The sacraments are not merely signs which Christ has guaranteed will somehow have an effect upon us. They are the actions of Christ; they are Christ giving life, Christ healing, Christ forgiving, Christ strengthening, Christ giving new powers and new responsibilities to the members of His Mystical Body, Christ worshiping His Father.

At the very heart of the sacramental system is Christ Himself in the sacrament of the Eucharist, from which all the sacraments radiate. It has been noted that prayer can be an action, like the action of Christ offering Himself on the cross in the supreme act of worship. The Eucharistic act, the Mass, is that supreme act of Christ prolonged in time and extended through space. The Mass, therefore, is the greatest prayer, the most sublime worship. In it Christ offers Himself to the Father and unites the members of His Mystical Body to Himself and to one another in Holy Communion.

To some it may seem odd that the Church should oblige her members to assist at Mass every Sunday under pain of mortal sin. The Church, they think, is unduly strict in this matter. Why make the obligation such a serious one? Why make failure to fulfill it a mortal sin? When one reflects a bit, however, one realizes that the Church is not acting unreasonably. She explicitly says that any serious inconvenience removes the obligation. But she insists that the obligation is in itself a most serious one simply because the Mass itself is so important. What is more reasonable that on the Lord's Day all the Lord's children should come together to worship the Father through Jesus Christ? We were made to worship God by nature and made a part of the "priestly people" by Baptism with a special power which enables us to take part in the supreme worship which Christ gives to the Father; what is more fitting, more necessary even, than that we gather as a family on the Lord's Day and take part in the Eucharist? Illness or anything which would present a serious difficulty would be enough to justify our absence, but not mere laziness or the desire for pleasure and recreation. The worship of God, especially the supreme worship which we give in the Mass, must come before rest and recreation. This is what the Church is saying when she obliges her children to offer Mass on Sundays and holy days under pain of serious sin.

It is not mere presence at Mass which the Church asks for. True, that is all she demands under sin, but she clearly desires more—that all take part in the Mass actively. She calls for participation in the Mass. The people, she tells us, are not to be a passive element at Mass, mere "dumb listeners," in the words of St. Pius X. The people have their part to play in this worship: they are to sing or recite aloud the parts of the Mass which belong to them, and to respond in word or song when the priest addresses them.

Catholic maturity shows itself here. The person who doesn't "go for all this participation" and insists on praying quietly, in his own way, alone in the crowd, does not understand what the Mass is. He is confusing private prayer, which one can do quite well alone, with liturgical prayer, which the family does together. He is clinging to old, familiar ways which are more to his liking, and has not examined his attitude to determine whether it squares with the meaning of the action of which he is objectively a part. He knows that it would be rude not to answer a neighbor who greeted him on the street, but he doesn't realize that this is exactly what he is doing when he remains silent as the priest says "*Dominus vobiscum*" to him; he wouldn't think of not joining in at a birthday party when everyone sings "Happy Birthday to You," but he doesn't stop to consider that he is doing just this when he remains silent as the rest of the congregation sings at Mass.

Some people try to justify their refusal to join in the prayers and the singing at Mass on the ground that they want to use their missal and say exactly the same words as the priest is saying. This attitude betrays a twofold misunderstanding. It shows ignorance of the Mass as family worship and ignorance of the diversity of function which exists in the Mass. There are some prayers and songs which belong to the priest; there are others which belong to the people. The man with his nose in the missal, trying to keep up with the priest in the prayers at the foot of the altar, is doing something which is not his job but that of the priest and servers. He would be participating much more properly if he were singing an entrance hymn or, at a high Mass, the Introit and Kyrie, as he is meant to do. The missal is fine if it is properly used, but when it interferes with proper participation it becomes a liability. The man who is silently reading his missal as the rest of the congregation is singing or praying together is like a man who would read a book during Thanksgiving dinner with the family. It is also odd to see people checking up for themselves, as it were, in their missals as the priest reads the Epistle and Gospel to them. This, too, is out of place. At this time the people should be listeners, not readers; they should be hearing the word of God, not reading it for themselves.

It is well known that in early times no one thought of separating the Mass from Communion, the eucharistic sacrificial offering from the eucharistic banquet which completes it. It was unthinkable to offer God a gift and refuse to accept the gift He offered in return, to join with the members of God's family in the great family act and refuse to take part in the banquet of love which united the members of the family more closely to Christ and to one another.

Later centuries saw a serious decline in liturgical awareness. How serious it was can be seen from the fact that the Church had to make a law obliging the faithful to receive Communion once a year, during the Easter season. People were anxious to look at the consecrated host, not to receive it. They lost sight of the fact that Communion is a family meal, and came to regard it as a purely personal matter between each individual and God. They thought of Communion as something apart from the Mass. Many preferred to receive before Mass in order that they might use the time of Mass for private thanksgiving. The heresy of Jansenism, which spread its pernicious influence through the Church in the eighteenth and nineteenth centuries, de-emphasized the humanity of Christ and made people afraid to receive Holy Communion. One was expected to obtain permission from one's confessor in order to receive Communion often. Confession was thought to be necessary before Communion at all times, not only in the case of mortal sin.

Eventually, Jansenism was condemned by the Church as the heresy it was, but its evil influence lived on. Even today it is noticeable. There are still many people who refuse to receive Communion at Mass unless they have been to confession the day before or at least within the week. There are still parents who tell their children, "I don't care what Father or Sister said—you must not receive Communion unless you go to confession first." The sad fact is that even today, with the teaching and preaching which is being done, most Catholics do not receive Communion every time they offer Mass. Sin accounts for some of these cases, of course, and breaking the eucharistic fast accounts for a few. But for the most part it is a case of dissociating the eucharistic sacrificial act from the eucharistic banquet. It is religious immaturity. A little questioning brings out this fact. When a priest asks penitent after penitent why he doesn't make Communion a part of his Sunday Mass, in most cases the answer is not "I keep falling into mortal sin and don't manage to get to confession" or "I like to have breakfast before Mass and don't want to wait three hours." The answer is the answer of a child: "I don't know."

Religious maturity requires a true appreciation of the sacraments and an awareness of their place in Christian life.

The sacraments are not just holy rites which are given at certain times in order to help us, and they are not merely fountains of grace; they are actions of Jesus Christ upon us. It is Christ Who acts through the sign of Baptism giving the Holy Spirit, the divine life and powers of the Christian. It is Christ Who forgives sin in the sacrament of Penance. It is Christ Who heals in the sacrament of Anointing of the Sick.

Our Lord remains among us in the Church. It is important to realize how much among us He is. He is not here in a static sense, merely present in the tabernacle; He is here in an intensely active sense. His presence in the Eucharist is an active one. Christ acts in the Eucharist by offering Himself and all His members to the Father in the Mass and by uniting us to Himself and to one another in Holy Communion. And His action in all the sacraments is connected with the Eucharist.

The sacraments do not exist in a vacuum. They are all part of the very life of a Christian, a life which centers about and is sustained by the Eucharist. In Baptism Christ gives a new life, a life which will be nourished by His body and blood, a life which will express itself above all in eucharistic worship. Baptism makes a person a member of the Body of Christ, an official worshiper, one who is to join with Christ and the other members of the Body in the Eucharist. In Confirmation, Christ gives an increased share in His priesthood, an increase in the power to participate in the Eucharist. In Penance, Christ restores the sinner to life and makes him worthy to rejoin the other members of the Body in the eucharistic banquet. In the Anointing of the Sick, Christ restores the sick members of His Body to health so that they may celebrate the Eucharist with the family. In marriage, Christ unites two of His members in a union of love which will be deepened day by day through the Eucharist. He unites them in order that they may bring forth new members of the Body, new children of God, who will take part in the Eucharist. In the priesthood, Christ gives, most wonderfully of all, the power of changing bread and wine into Him.

The sacraments, therefore, are not simply prayers and rites which are performed for the sake of an individual, nor are they even simply the actions of Christ on an individual. They are Christ's actions on a member of His Mystical Body which concern that member's relationship to the Body and to the other members of the Body. This great fact was sensed by the sick woman who asked to be anointed in church with her fellow parishioners present. It was definitely not understood by another woman, a godmother at a Baptism, who said, "Oh, good! We're the only ones."

Actually, it would be most fitting—although obviously impossible except in very small communities—to administer Baptism with the whole parish present to welcome the new members into the Mystical Body. Something like this takes place when converts are baptized at the Easter Vigil, and it is most meaningful. There are parishes in which Baptism is administered immediately after the last Mass on Sunday, and the congregation is invited to remain. Some parishes issue a general invitation to the Baptism of converts at the end of an inquiry class. Others encourage parents to invite their friends and relatives to take part in the actual Baptism, not only in the party which is held afterwards in the home. Now that it is possible to give the rite of Baptism to adults in several stages, as was done in earlier centuries, some parishes have adopted the practice of performing the initial ceremonies at the time of the sermon at Sunday Mass, with the whole congregation joining in, saying the amens and reciting the Creed and the Lord's Prayer together.

What is true of Baptism is true also of the other sacraments. Each confirmation and each marriage is the concern of the whole Christian community. In practice, of course, only the friends and relatives can be present, but ideally the whole parish should be there with their fellow members of Christ's Body at these important moments in their lives. It is becoming more and more common for the bridal couple to invite their friends to receive Holy Communion at their wedding. This practice is most fitting. Some bishops ordain young men to the priesthood in their own parish church so that the new priest's friends and neighbors, the people of the community in which he grew up, can share in the joy of his ordination.

When it is said that the sacraments are social rather than merely individual in nature, one apparent exception comes to mind—the sacrament of Penance. The privacy of the confessional, the whispered confession, and the secrecy to which the priest is bound all seem to indicate a purely personal matter, something which concerns this individual penitent and no one else. Yet the sacrament of Penance also is social. It concerns this individual penitent not as an isolated individual but in his relationship to the whole Body of Christ. If the sinner was an isolated individual, he would not need to go through the Church, would not have to confess his sins to a priest. All he would have to do would be to express his sorrow to God. This, of course, is precisely the point which Protestants raise. They see no reason at all for bringing the priest into the picture. "Why not simply confess your sins to God, as we do?" they ask. The answer is that Catholics do confess their sins to God and ask His pardon, but that since they are members of a family, the Church, they must also go through the family and be reconciled to God through it when they have injured the family by committing serious sin.

It is important to remember that the only time the Church obliges her children to confess to a priest is when they have committed mortal sin. She encourages and advises all to receive the sacrament of Penance often, but that is another matter. There is no obligation, even at Easter time, for those who have not sinned seriously. The reason the Church acts this way, as we said above, is that a member of the Church who sins seriously does an injury to the whole family. Even when the sin is not publicly known, the Church is affected, for the holiness of the whole Body has been diminished to the extent that one member has lost the divine life. This member, who should be contributing to the good of the whole Body, has rendered himself useless by his sins; as long as he remains in that state his prayers and actions are of no value. He does not have the divine life, and therefore none of his actions have merit in the sight of God. Supernaturally, he is dead; he is dead weight, a liability rather than an asset to the family. The family has a right, therefore, to require him to make peace with God. This he does by going through the family, that is, by confessing his sins to an official representative of the family, the priest. Then, reconciled to God and to God's whole family, the repentant sinner is worthy to rejoin the Christian community at the banquet table of the Lord.

The ancient practice of public penance by members of

the Church brought out this idea very clearly. People who were guilty of such sins as open adultery or public repudiation of the faith could not simply confess their sins secretly to any priest and receive absolution immediately. They were required to do public penance all during Lent before they were absolved from their sins and permitted to rejoin the faithful in the celebration of the Eucharist. On Ash Wednesday these public penitents confessed their sins to the bishop. They put on sackcloth and ashes, and did not enter church on the Lord's Day with the rest of the community but remained outside, at the door of the church, while Mass was celebrated. On Holy Thursday, when the whole community was gathered in church, these public penitents were conducted into the presence of the bishop. There, before the whole assembly, the bishop gave them absolution from their sins. Thereupon they put off their sackcloth and, dressed in ordinary clothes, rejoined the community and took part once more in the celebration of the Eucharist.

This ancient practice might seem unduly severe today, but it succeeded in giving a dramatic expression of the Church's attitude toward serious sin and the way it affects the whole family of God. In the days of public penance the Church did not require those whose sins were not known to submit to this ordeal, and today she does not require it of anyone. But her attitude toward serious sin is the same: it is something which injures the whole family.

The Church does not put herself between the sinner and God by requiring a sinner to confess to a priest. In the first place, the Church *is* Christ, the Mystical Christ, binding and loosing as the Master instructed her to do. In the second place, the Church is not interfering with God's mercy and delaying His forgiveness; on the contrary, she tells the sinner that God will forgive any sin immediately, as soon as the sinner is sorry because of love of God and resolves to be reconciled to the family.

Since the days of public penance the practice has arisen of using the sacrament of Penance not as a matter of necessity but simply as a means of overcoming daily faults and making progress in the spiritual life. It has become common for people to go to confession to confess venial sins. The sacrament of Penance has come to be seen not only as the "second plank after shipwreck" but also as a divinely established means of growth in holiness. This is the origin of what is known as the confession of devotion, so universally practiced throughout the Church today. The confession of devotion is more an individual matter than the confession of necessity, by which a sinner is reconciled to the family. Yet even the confession of devotion cannot be divorced from the part which each member plays in the life and work of the Body of Christ. We work out our salvation and grow in holiness not as isolated individuals but as members of the Church. The sacrament of Penance is one of the means Christ uses to make the members of His Church holier and thus increase the holiness of the Church itself. Used properly, the confession of devotion is a great help in forming more zealous, more apostolic, more mature members of the Mystical Body.

Many people confuse the confession of devotion with the confession of necessity, thinking they must go to confession before they receive Communion even though they have committed only venial sins. They also think that they are required to confess every venial sin according to kind and number, as would be the case with mortal sins. This confusion may well arise from the way children are trained for their first Communion. The usual procedure is to have the children go to confession for the first time a day or two before they make their first Communion. Thus the impression is given, despite what Sister and Father say, that there is a connection between confession and Communion, even when there is no mortal sin. Furthermore, children are taught to confess all their venial sins according to kind and number. The model confession which is offered as a guide goes something like this: "Bless me, Father, for I have sinned. This is my first confession. I lied eight times. I disobeyed six times. I fought twice. I swore three times. I laughed and talked in church once. I stole four times." No sister or priest would teach a child that there is an obligation to confess all one's venial sins, much less according to kind and number. Nevertheless, in practice, children are given to know that this is what they are expected to do. The result is that years later, in adult life, it is the same story: "I lied five times. I was angry three times. I swore six times. I used bad language ten times. I took God's name in vain three times. I missed my morning prayers six times and my evening prayers twice"—and so on, and so on.

What is wrong with this? It makes for routine confessions; it leads to a rather mechanical attitude toward confession; the emphasis is on the matter to be forgiven rather than on the purpose of amendment. A great deal of care has been taken to put everything on the list, but how much care has been taken to prepare for an encounter with Christ? How much thought has there been about a real effort to eliminate one or two real faults and to practice a particular virtue? In the case of a confession of necessity, care must be taken to include every mortal sin. This care is an indication of the sincerity of the confession. The same kind of care exercised in the confession of devotion has the effect of dissipating thought and energy and preventing concentration on the real purpose of the confession.

The sacrament of Penance is not needed for the forgiveness of venial sins. Why, then, should we confess any of them? Why go to confession at all if we have no mortal sins to confess? The answer is that the sacrament of Penance, being an encounter with Christ, is a great and powerful means of helping us to overcome our faults and to grow in holiness. The confession of devotion looks more to the future than to the past. The penitent comes not so much to receive pardon for past faults as to ask Christ's help to keep from committing these faults in the future. He confesses his faults to Christ because he seeks the sacramental contact. He wants to declare to Christ Himself his shortcomings and his failures to love as much as he should. He wants to receive sacramental absolution for these faults and sacramental aid in overcoming them in the future.

If this is the aim of the penitent who tries to confess all his venial sins, well and good. But from the standpoint of progress would it not be better to mention only one or two faults, those for which one is especially sorry and on which one is really working? Too often penitents return week after week with the same sins in the same order and even in the same numbers. If they would sincerely ask themselves, "What fault does God want me to concentrate on? What is the thing which more than anything else is preventing me from loving God as I ought to love Him?" they would get out of the rut; their confessions would be more meaningful and more fruitful. They would be working earnestly on a particular problem, and so would the graces of the sacrament.

The priest, too, would find it easier to help. It is difficult for a confessor to give advice when the penitent has come forth with seven or eight species of venial sins. A priest is much more capable of offering helpful advice when a penitent names a particular fault for which he is especially sorry. Here numbers can be helpful. The same kind of exactitude as in the case of mortal sins is not expected, but it makes a lot of difference whether one says "I lied" or "I lied six times this week." The latter is more likely to indicate to both the priest and the penitent that it is advisable to do something about the situation. It is very helpful, too, for both the penitent and the confessor if mention is made of the reason why a certain sin was committed. If the penitent says, for example, "I lied because I wanted to appear big in the eyes of others," he and the confessor will both realize that the problem is not only untruthfulness but also pride. If the penitent says, "I stole because I was thinking of myself rather than the good of my neighbor," both will see clearly that charity is involved as well as justice.

At the other extreme from the penitent who feels he must confess every venial sin is the man who can find nothing at all to tell the priest. This, of course, is a case not of sanctity but rather of insensitivity. What this man needs is to be awakened to the meaning of the Christian life. He is the kind who thinks that as long as he has not committed murder or adultery or missed Mass on Sunday, he is doing just fine. He needs to learn what loving God and loving one's neighbor really mean in terms of daily life. A good confessor can help a person like this to spiritual maturity only if the person really desires to achieve it.

We have said several times that the sacraments are part of the worship of the Church. Yet it is doubtful whether the average Catholic thinks of the sacraments as worship at all. He sees them rather as one-way streets by which God gives grace to us. The sacraments are assuredly channels of grace, but they are also worship; man also praises God and gives to God in the sacraments. An examination of the prayers which are part of the ritual of Baptism or Last Anointing, for example, shows very clearly how the sacraments are worship. And once again, the sacrament of Penance, at first sight might seem to be an exception, but it is not.

First of all, the reception of the sacrament of Penance entails a visit to the church, a genuflection, the sign of the cross, and prayer. After an Act of Contrition comes the examination of conscience. Then follows an act which Catholics do matter-of-factly but which is in itself something wonderful—the act of entering a confessional, kneeling down, and confessing one's sins to a priest. Although we don't advert to it as such, this is a great act of worship. It is an expression of faith, an acceptance of the fact that God has given the power of forgiving sins to the Church and that in the darkness of the confessional there will be an encounter with Christ Himself. Hope, too, is evident in the penitent's confident expectation that God in His mercy will forgive his sins in this sacrament. The humility the penitent manifests strikes many people outside the Church with awe.

The sacrament is also an expression of love, contained in the penitent's expression of sorrow for his sin. Finally, the sacrament entails an expression of obedience in that a penance is accepted and obediently executed. When one comes to think of it, it is astonishing how much worship is given to God in connection with the reception of the sacrament of Penance. Here is a thought for the man who doesn't go to confession often because he has "nothing to tell": he might go to give rather than just to get.

A realization that one worships God in receiving the sacraments should lead to better reception. If I go not merely to receive but also to give, I am apt to prepare myself better. Paradoxically, I will then actually receive more grace. The essential graces of a sacrament are given automatically, as all Catholics know. This very fact can lead to passive, mechanical reception if one is not careful. It is necessary to keep in mind that a more fruitful reception requires activity on the part of the recipient. In fact, the very expression "to *receive* a sacrament" is not a very happy one. It is true that an infant merely receives Baptism passively, but a person who has reached the age of reason should not only come to the sacrament with his heart wide open for his encounter with Christ but also be active himself as he experiences the action of Christ.

It is odd, really, that we speak of "receiving" Holy Communion. Communion is rather something into which we *enter*. In order to have a correct and mature attitude toward the sacraments, we must stress the part we play and not overemphasize the undeniable fact that the sacraments work automatically. In order to receive the sacraments as we should, gaining the greatest profit for ourselves and giving the greatest worship to God, we must prepare ourselves to receive them, stir up our faith, hope, and love, desire the graces which Christ is waiting to give us, and be ready to use those graces in our daily lives.

The best preparation for the Eucharist is the practice of charity beforehand and a full and active participation in the Mass. The best thanksgiving afterwards is an attempt to cooperate with the graces we have received to help us love our neighbor and imitate Christ in our daily actions. The best preparation in the case of Penance is to stir up real sorrow for our failure to love enough, and the best thanksgiving is to make a real effort to overcome the temptation to fall back into the particular sins we have confessed. In order to give to God the worship we should give in the sacraments and to receive the full benefit we should obtain from them, we must see the sacraments as vital to Christian living and relate our lives to them.

6

Not Without Guidance

"Father, I'd like to see the movie that is playing tonight at the Bijou. What does the Church say about it?"

The priest did something he had thought people did only in the movies: he looked at the telephone receiver in astonishment as if it were the face of the man at the other end of the line. An outlandish picture flashed before his mind. He could see the pope in solemn session with all the bishops and cardinals, ankle-deep in newspapers and magazines, seriously studying what movie was playing at various theaters all over the world and making pronouncements about each of them.

The priest found the question depressing. The man was not calling to see what rating the picture had before he allowed his children to see it. He was asking for himself. Here was a man who actually sought to be treated like a child, a man who was so unsure of himself that he wanted others to make judgments for him, even in such minor matters as what movies he should see. Here was a man who had been taught as a child that he must obey lawful authority but who had never come to appreciate the real meaning and purpose of obedience and authority.

The fourth commandment obliges us to obey all lawful authority—that of parents, the Church, the government. It also obliges us to use authority rightly. But the fourth commandment does not aim at keeping those who must obey authority in a state of immaturity—quite to the contrary; one of the purposes of authority is to liberate people and bring them to maturity. Neither does this commandment aim at providing justification for would-be tyrants in any of the areas of authority. Maturity requires an appreciation of the real meaning of authority and obedience. The mature Christian practices the virtue of obedience with intelligence and charity, and exercises what authority he is called upon to exercise in the same way.

In practicing obedience one is not expected to cease to use one's mind or strip oneself of all desires and inclinations. St. Francis of Assisi once asked a young friar whether he would like to go to the Holy Land as a missionary. The young man replied that he did not know. St. Francis was astonished. He asked the friar why he could say neither yes nor no. The friar replied that he could have no preference until he knew what St. Francis wanted him to do. This young friar was obedient, to be sure, but he was hardly acting in a human way.

A priest who was singing a high Mass in a convent chapel one morning heard, amid the singing voices, one flat voice which spoke the responses loudly instead of singing them. Later he had occasion to ask the nonsinger why it was she was so obviously out of step with the others. She replied that Mother Superior had told her to say the altar boy's responses in a loud voice at Mass. This religious, too, was surely obedient, but hardly in an intelligent way. She failed to use her own mind even to the extent of making the obvious conclusion that singing the responses was just as valid as reciting them.

The virtue of obedience is not a matter of unthinking subservience. It is not a posture which degrades the human person by depriving him of his rationality and his freedom. An act of obedience should be a human act, prompted by love and free, a commitment of oneself for a reason which the person who obeys recognizes and with which he wholeheartedly agrees. To be a virtue, obedience presupposes an acceptance of the right of authority to command. Obedience and authority are two sides of the same coin. If Johnny must turn off the television and go to bed when he is told to, there must be someone who has the right to tell him to do these things. And this right to command obedience comes ultimately from God. Far from being a sterile and unreasoning compliance, therefore, obedience should be an act of love. It is God Whom we obey when we obey lawful authority.

God shares His authority with men in order to insure order in the world, to provide protection for the rights of all, and to help His children develop to full maturity. Nothing could be more blasphemous than to picture God as a tyrant Who imposes His will ruthlessly on men, forcing all to do what He wants them to and eager to destroy in His vengeance anyone who dares cross Him or refuses to bend to His will. God is love. He created man not to force His will on him but to bring him to everlasting life, to a share in the happiness of the Blessed Trinity. God created man with a free will not in order to test him but in order that man might develop into what God knows will be truly himself.

God wants each of His children to be his own unique self. Rubber-stamp conformity is the furthest thing from the ideal of God. He Who makes each snowflake different from all the others loves variety and individuality in His children. He wanted one Francis of Assisi, one Curé of Ars, one Mary Magdalene. He wants each of His children to be a saint, and each a unique saint. As a wise and loving Father Who sees that each of his children is different and helps each develop according to his own powers, God is eager for each of His children to mature in his own way.

But God does more than see the differences in His children: He is responsible for those differences. God sees His children in somewhat the same way a landscaper sees the materials he begins with. Looking at a sapling, he sees a full-grown tree. Looking at a handful of seeds, he sees a green lawn. God, looking at any of His children, sees that person in his fully developed state, fully redeemed by Christ, fully sanctified, fully grown to the state of perfection and glory for which God intends him. And He will bring him to this state gently, guiding him to develop the powers which He has put into him.

In order for a man to accomplish this growth to perfection, God has created him with a free will. He has redeemed him, giving him Christ's life, giving him the Holy Spirit, to fashion him in Christ's image. And as an aid in this growth to perfection, God shares with men his fatherly authority. Its aim is not to crush him, not to stifle his initiative, not to enslave him, but quite to the contrary, to liberate him. Its aim is to develop him in the use of his powers to the point of true freedom, to guide him to maturity, to lead him to the stage where he will act according to the benevolent will of his loving Father, not because he must but because he wants to.

Parents who fulfill their role properly act as instruments of God, helping and guiding their children to full maturity. The mature Christian parent knows that God has given him authority over his children precisely because the children are not capable of making prudent decisions as yet and have to be directed. The good parent knows that it is his role to help the child until he is able to make his own decisions and lead his own life.

The two extremes of misuse of parental authority are very well known. One is exemplified by the parent who fails to use his authority and lets a child have his own way, even to his own detriment. Such was the case with the Catholic mother who explained why her eight-year-old daughter was not attending the Catholic school: "She doesn't seem to want to go there. She prefers the public school." At the other extreme are the tyrannical parent who enjoys the power he has and dominates his children, the overprotective parent who makes every decision for his children and does not allow them to develop prudence and initiative, and the selfish parent, usually female, who binds her children to her so tightly that they just can't bear to marry and leave mother. The parent who is mature himself aims to teach his children to stand up, to walk, and then to walk away.

The Christian husband who is truly mature understands the meaning of St. Paul's words, "Let wives be subject to their husbands as to the Lord; because a husband is head of the wife, just as Christ is head of the Church, being himself savior of the body" (Eph 5:22–24). The mature Christian man accepts and exercises the authority that is his by nature as head of the family, but he does not exercise this authority in a tyrannical way. He knows that St. Paul goes on to say, "Husbands, love your wives, just as Christ also loved the Church, and delivered himself up for her. . . . Even thus ought husbands also to love their wives as their own bodies" (Eph 5:25, 28). The relationship between husband and wife, of which St. Paul speaks here, is not a brutal or slavish subjection of the wife to the husband, but the relationship of one who is loved to her lover. The Christian husband is to exercise his authority in partnership with his wife, taking her wishes into consideration, even when he must make the final decision himself.

In American society, the old-time authoritarian husband and father has pretty well vanished from the scene—the man whose word was law and whose orders were given without explanation or consultation and obeyed by all without question. Nowadays, when a husband receives an invitation to join the boys for poker or golf, in most cases he consults his wife before accepting, to see whether she has any previous plans. As a rule, he does not come home from work expecting to be waited on hand and foot. Very often he helps out by putting the children to bed, sometimes even by giving his wife a hand with the dishes. This is not necessarily an indication that the husband has abdicated as head of the family, as some complain; it is as often a sign of real Christian maturity on the part of a husband who is so sure of himself and of his authority as head of the family that he does not hesitate to act in a loving and considerate way, as St. Paul teaches he should.

Some must use authority because of the very office they

have—a bishop in his diocese, for example, or a judge in his court. Others must use authority because it has been conferred on them by a group. These people, too, have an obligation to exercise their authority in a mature and Christian manner.

We have pointed out that one of the purposes of authority is to help people mature; the other is to help a group of people achieve a common end. It is obvious that in any group there must be leadership. People have different ideas about what should be done and how it should be done. Observe a group of amateur mechanics with their heads under the hood of a stalled car, and see how many different ideas there can be about a relatively simple problem. Listen to speeches on the floor of Congress, and see how many differences of opinion there can be about problems that are really complex. Whenever a group of men assembles for some purpose, it usually chooses a leader to coordinate its activities. Even five highly trained professional basketball players need a floor captain. In a group, since each person is free to have his own opinions and since each, drawing on his own experience, may judge things differently from the others, someone must be given authority to see that a common decision is reached and carried out. This authority implies the ability to make decisions and enforce them. There are many ways in which decisions can be enforced, but a man in a position of leadership who is unable to enforce them does not really have authority, regardless of his position.

The authority which leadership in a group entails appears in many forms. The man who runs a business is a leader and has authority over his employees. The foreman of a crew has authority over his men. The president of a parish society has a certain amount of authority. Even the leader of a study club or discussion group has authority. In each case the leader, as a mature Christian, is to exercise his authority with prudence and charity in order to bring to the whole group the benefits which the members seek. The leader of a section of the Christian Family Movement, for example, must see to it that everyone has the opportunity of expressing himself, that no one is allowed to dominate the discussion, and that the various parts of the meeting are in proportion and in line with the purpose of the movement, the apostolic formation of each member.

It is apparent that authority must be used in different ways, according to the circumstances. There are situations which demand that someone take charge and give orders which must be obeyed at once. At a fire, the fire chief issues commands; it would hardly do for the fireman to sit down and hold a meeting in democratic fashion to determine the best way of putting out the fire. Other situations, however, are best met by a discussion in which suggestions are welcomed, grievances aired, and a decision reached which takes into account the ideas of the whole group.

In the old days, when the philosophy of rugged individualism ruled, a boss often enough hired and fired at will and made all the decisions himself, without consulting anyone else. Few businesses are run that way today. It is generally recognized that efficiency is greater when responsibility is shared, and that a policy can be criticized without thereby criticizing the boss if the policy has been determined by a whole committee. Even the military, a classic example of authority and obedience, is today undergoing what is called the fraternalization of authority. Where once there was merely an order, given without any explanation and demanding prompt, unquestioning obedience, there is now much more effort to obtain efficiency and wholehearted cooperation by means of explanation and consultation. Men in the army today have greater responsibility, and they are expected to think for themselves to an extent that shocks some of the old-timers, who are used to the strict, almost inhuman discipline of bygone days.

In the Western world today, with the growing fraternalization of authority and men's natural and proper indignation at the totalitarianism which exists in certain parts of the world, there is resentment in some quarters of an institution which claims to have authority which is no less than divine —the Catholic Church. Millions of Catholics accept that claim and willingly give obedience to the Church.

Many people outside the Church look askance at the attitude of Catholics. In this age of democracy, they regard the Church as an anachronism, a holdover from feudalism, an authoritarian institution which is in contradiction to the modern idea of freedom. Some have strong feelings on this matter. They think that Catholics are held in bondage by the hierarchy and told what they may and may not think or do in all matters, ranging from what they must believe about the nature of God all the way down to whom they must vote for in a local election. They point out the Galileo case and the Spanish Inquisition, and on the contemporary scene they wax indignant over the index of forbidden books and the Legion of Decency. There are also people to whom these critics can point as proof of their contention—the omniscient pastor who regards his parishioners as sheep, mindless, mute, passive, not to be trusted with any responsibility; the ecclesiastic who says, "The laity are children, and children are to be seen and not heard"; the layman who is genuinely shocked to find an article in a Catholic periodical which disagrees with an opinion expressed by a churchman; the Catholic who expects the Church to give him a critique of every book and movie. All these serve to strengthen the conviction in the minds of many outside the Church that the Church is not a mother but a tyrannical matriarch, a dictatorial institution that is out of place in the twentieth century.

In any discussion of authority and obedience in the Church a clarification must be made at the outset—what is meant by the word *Church* in the context. When we say that the Church teaches that there are three persons in one God, we are speaking of the Church in her official capacity as teacher, the Holy Father, and the whole apostolic college exercising the mandate of Christ Himself to go and teach all nations and speaking with the authority of Christ. When we say that the Church teaches that the souls in Purgatory can aid us by their prayers, we are speaking merely of an opinion which is commonly held by Catholic theologians. When it is said that the Church favors the union of Church and state, what is meant is simply that this traditional position is still held by some high-ranking prelates and theologians in the Church; it is by no means universally held by bishops, cardinals, and theologians within the Church. For some Catholics—the man on the phone, for example, who wants the Church's opinion of a certain movie—"the Church" is any priest, just as for some people outside the Church it is any Catholic. Often enough one hears it said,

"Oh, I know the Church teaches that anyone who is not a Catholic cannot be saved. A Catholic told me so."

What is the Church? St. Paul makes it very plain: the Church is Christ; it is the Mystical Body of Christ. This Body is made up of all the members of the Church, from the pope down to the infant who was baptized last Sunday afternoon. There are many ways of describing the Church. She is the Bride of Christ; she is the flock of Christ. But St. Paul's description of the Church as the Body of Christ illustrates best, perhaps, the unity and diversity which exist within the Church. The Church is all who are within the Church, not merely the pope or the bishops or the priests; she is the union of all the faithful in Christ.

But this Church is both a visible and a hierarchical Church. There is within her a great diversity of functions. The Church is Christ, living and teaching and sanctifying today. Christ does these things in and through all the members of His Church, but not in the same way. Christ teaches some of the members of His Body through their parents, teachers, and others who share in the teaching mission of His Church. He teaches all the members of His Body through those whom He has officially made successors of the apostles, the hierarchy. This is a basic point of Catholic belief. Catholics could never agree with the idea that the Church is a democracy in which everyone has equal authority. They believe very firmly that the Church is hierarchical. An understanding of this word is necessary if one is to understand the meaning of authority and obedience in the Church. Cardinal Cushing of Boston gives a good explanation of this important term in his pastoral letter "The Church and Public Opinion."

Our Lord, we must remember, is the perfect Mediator between his heavenly Father and sinful mankind. This means that Our Lord is mankind's authentic high priest. The work of his priesthood was the redemption of the world. The Church prolongs the priestly mission of her divine Founder. All the members of the Church share in the same blessing. All pursue the same goals. Not all, to be sure, enjoy the same powers, nor are all qualified to perform the same function.

To say it in other words, all the members of the Church participate in the priestly mission of the Church, but differently, according to the sacraments which they have received.

Within a diocese the pastoral charge rests upon the bishop. This responsibility serves to remind the bishop that he is an apostle; he is not merely an administrator, nor just an ecclesiastical functionary, but a missionary. He is the judge and doctor of the faith. He is the father of the priesthood in his diocese. He governs the Church in the name of Christ and after the example of Christ. His authority reveals itself in service, a service, a service which finds its exemplar in the washing of the disciples' feet, as summed up in the Gospel passage: "Let him who is greatest among you become as the youngest; and him who is the chief as the servant" (Lk 22:26).

The bishop shares his pastoral charge both with his priests and with the faithful of his diocese, but he shares it differently in each case. Because the bishop is not intended to fulfill the obligations of his pastoral charge by himself, he ordains men to the priesthood and gives to them a very specific share in his apostolic mission. Priests are cooperators in the bishop's order. They participate in his priesthood. They share in the ministry of the word. They assist the bishop in the government of the diocese.

The bishop also shares his pastoral charge with the faithful. Through Baptism, the layman begins to share in the life of Christ. This life is redemptive and involves the salvation of all men. Thus through Baptism, and in a special way through the sacrament of Confirmation, the layman makes his own the life and cares of the Church—as the Church extends in time the pastoral charge of the Lord Himself. Whether we consider the layman "in his home life with all its family problems," or in his professional life "with all its technical problems," or in "his earthly citizenship with all its economic and political problems," we can always apply to him this same sharing in the life of the Church. . . . The layman's role in the hierarchy's pastoral charge is not some optional right, it is a pastoral imperative. It is only in the perspective of this imperative that we can set the stage for the role of public opinion within God's Church. The formation and expression of public opinion is one of the many duties of the layman in the life of the Mystical Body.*

Cardinal Cushing is stressing the fact that while the Church is unquestionably hierarchical, she is incomparably more than merely a juridical institution. To concentrate on only the juridical aspect of the Church would be to give a picture which is as unattractive as it is untrue. Father Yves Congar gives an example of this sort of thing. He quotes a statement made in a public address: "The Church is given the task of feeding the flock of Christ." This change of meaning is serious, Congar says; the Church herself is the flock of Christ. The speaker is identifying the Church with the priestly government or even simply with that government's Roman courts. Congar points out that this idea of the Church is out of keeping with Scriptural, patristic, and liturgical usage. It runs the risk of separating the Church from the sphere in which men are trained in the spiritual life. Congar further says that this purely juridical idea of the Church favors the growth of the notions that the priest governs his parish, the bishop and Pope are judges, the Pope is a sovereign, and the Church is *queen of mankind* rather than mother.

Actually, the Church is the whole family of God, the holy and "priestly people," as it is expressed in the Mass.

* Richard Cardinal Cushing, "The Church and Public Opinion," pamphlet, pp. 8–11.

The traditional emphasis has always been on the idea of family or flock rather than on the idea of the stole and its subjects. The priest who is in charge of a parish is called pastor, which means shepherd; so is the bishop of a diocese. The word *pope* means father, and the Pope calls himself "the servant of the servants of God." The relationship of all within the Church is a family relationship. The people call their priests *father* and look to their bishop and to the Pope for paternal guidance.

At the same time, all in the Church are children of the Church—the priests, the bishops, and the Pope as well as the people. All learn from the Church, even those who teach. The Holy Father has the power of making an infallible pronouncement right out of the blue, without any research or preparation, but he would sin seriously against prudence were he to do so. He is expected to consult theologians and to search the heart of the Church to see what Catholic faith is on the subject. And while the relationship of fatherhood and sonship exists between the clergy and the laity, at the same time all in the Church are brothers.

The people of a parish, even people who are old enough to be the priest's parents, call their pastor *father*. This title is apt. The priest feeds them in the Eucharist; he is their spiritual father in the confessional; he preaches the word of God to them; he is the leader in the family act of worship, the Mass. But it does not follow that the people are children who must depend on the priest for everything. Some of them may be better educated than the priest himself. There may be architects, lawyers, accountants, psychiatrists, artists, and others in the parish who know a great deal more than the priest in certain fields; some even may know more theology than he does. There surely are people with ordinary jobs who are nonetheless intelligent and well educated. These people are not children in the sense that they should be "seen and not heard." If they are children of the Church, so is the priest whom they call *father*.

In speaking of the authority of the Church, an important distinction must be kept in mind—the distinction between the teaching of the Church and her power of ruling and guiding. In both the Church has and exercises authority, but in different ways.

First, the Church is infallible when she teaches officially on matters of faith and morals. Catholics accept what the Church teaches in this way as a matter of faith. The Pope and the bishops accept and believe everything the Church teaches just as do the lay people. Even on matters which fall within the scope of their teaching office but in which infallibility is not invoked, the Pope and the bishops speak with the greatest authority. When they are thus giving the teachings of the Church on a matter of faith or morals, those teachings are to be accepted as matters of faith, and the acceptance is required by the virtue of faith.

Second, the Church will always be our mother and our teacher. She was commissioned to teach all nations by Christ Himself. In fact, the Church is Christ Himself, teaching the eternal truths which He teaches. Therefore, the Church speaks "as one having authority, and not as the Scribes and Pharisees." Some people are shocked at the assurances which the Church shows in her teaching. They are outraged at her claim to be infallible in matters of faith and morals. But Catholics realize that without this assurance, without this infallibility, the Church would not be the safe teacher she is. They do not feel they are confined in an intellectual prison, as some outside the Church allege. They know that what the Church teaches them is truth, and that the effect of that teaching is not to restrain the mind but to liberate it. Far from discouraging thought and speculation, the Church is the champion of the intellect and encourages investigation and study in every field, including, of course, theology.

There have been times when churchmen have acted in a repressive and reactionary way regarding intellectual pursuits, to be sure. But these are incidents, not a matter of policy. The consistent movement of the Church has always been in the direction of progress. She has always urged men to develop the powers which God has given them and utilize the world over which God has made man lord. Her aim is to promote a more excellent life for all in this world while preparing men for their final destiny, eternal life in Heaven. The encyclicals of all the recent popes give abundant evidence of this aim. If Catholics are not leaders in science, art, and philosophy, it is not because they are good Catholics. Whatever the reason for any failure in this regard, it cannot be denied that Catholics would be better Catholics, truer to their heritage, more perfect sons of the Church, if they were leaders in their fields. There has been much soul-searching in recent years by Catholics, especially educators, over the problem of lack of proportionate Catholic representation in the field of science in the United States. This concern is significant, for it implies a recognition that such a state of affairs is not normal or desirable.

Some people outside the Church think that because the Church teaches infallibly on matters of faith and morals and all Catholics accept the Church's teaching, Catholics all think alike on every question. Anyone with any knowledge of Catholics or the Church knows how false this notion is. Catholics differ widely in their opinions. There are Catholic liberals and Catholic conservatives, and representatives of every shade of political opinion between. There are different ideas of how the Church's teaching should be applied to concrete situations among Catholics on many issues, as there is and should be among any people who enjoy intellectual freedom.

Converts often express their amazement at the intellectual freedom which they find within the Church, having shared the idea, before they really knew the Church, which many outside the Church have—that the Pope is forever coming out with infallible pronouncements and that consequently there is little or no room for opinion within the Church. Actually, only two clearly infallible pronouncements have been made in the last hundred years. This is not to say that the Church does not teach with the greatest authority on other matters, but the official teaching of the Church covers an area which is not nearly so great as is usually imagined. Beyond this area is a vast realm in which all sorts of different opinions, speculations, and sometimes very lively controversies flourish. Sometimes what is pretty generally regarded as an official teaching of the Church turns out on investigation to be merely a theological opinion or a matter of possible private revelation, of which the Church says only that it contains nothing contrary to faith and that consequently one is free to believe it if one wishes to.

It is often said that one can go to a Catholic church anywhere in the world and be sure of hearing the same doctrine preached from the pulpit. This is true in the sense that Catholic doctrine is taught and believed throughout the whole Church; Catholics do not disagree about any actual teaching of the Church. However, not everything which is uttered in a pulpit in a Catholic church is Catholic doctrine. Pious legends, private revelations, and theological opinions can sometimes be heard in sermons. They should be put forth as such by the preacher, but at times they are not. A case in point is that of a priest who used as an introduction to his sermon the story of an apparition of our Lady. He began with the flat statement that on a certain day in a certain year a young girl, walking through a forest in France, came upon a lady dressed all in white and weeping. The lady revealed that she was the Mother of God and that her arms were getting tired from her efforts to hold back the avenging hand of her divine Son. The preacher did not say that this vision and the remarkable message which allegedly accompanied it were matters of faith, but dressed as he was in surplice and stole and standing in a pulpit in a Catholic church, he must have given many in the congregation the impression that this was the teaching of the Church. In reality, of course, this was only a private matter which each member of the congregation was free to accept or reject on the basis of the evidence as he saw it.

The message in this case, with its odd imputation of wrath to Christ, might well give pause to the thoughtful hearer. It could trouble him deeply to think that this was the doctrine of the Church. Of course, the man in the pew is not supposed to be sitting there with a critical attitude, ready to disagree with what he hears from the pulpit. People come to hear a sermon in order to hear the word of God. The proper attitude is reverence, receptiveness, and docility. We listen humbly and receive spiritual nourishment. Even those who are better educated than the preacher may benefit from his sermon; scholars and bishops used to come to hear the simple and holy Curé of Ars preach. However, a sermon does not have the same authority as a papal encyclical, and a mature Catholic will be able to distinguish between the doctrine of the Church and the opinion of a priest, speaking in or out of the pulpit. The old priest who says that you have to believe that God made the world in six days is speaking for himself, not for the Church. So is the priest who is opposed to the idea of aid to underdeveloped countries; the encyclical *Christianity and Social Progress* makes the Church's teaching on this point very clear.

The Church was commissioned by Christ not only to teach but also to rule in His name. Therefore, the Church exercises her authority also in an area in which not the virtue of faith but the virtue of obedience is involved.

As for the laws which the Church makes for her members, it should be obvious that they are designed to ensure that her members do what they should do and need to do. They are concerned with worship and penance and mortification, all of which are necessary in the spiritual life. But the Church, like a good mother, is not interested merely in obtaining obedience to these laws; she is trying to train her children to the practice of penance and self-denial. She is not content to have Catholics simply go on blindly obeying her laws as they did when they were eight years old; she wants them to live according to the spirit of these laws and to fast and do penance not only on Fridays but also at other times, on their own, because of conviction. The Church is not interested in filling the church building again and again on Sunday in order to crack the whip over Catholics or to "show the Protestants" or, as a cynic might say, to get that money in the collection basket, but wants to guide her members to a full appreciation of their primary function as part of a priestly people. She wants to develop in them the virtue of religion. The Church uses her authority not to keep people in line, not to show who is boss, but to bring about the sanctification of her members. She is not content with an external observation, a mere keeping of the letter of the law. She desires a response dictated by love, since what she seeks is growth in the spiritual life.

The bishop in his diocese is the apostle of Jesus Christ, and thus represents Christ to his people. His task is both teaching and ruling that portion of Christ's flock which has been committed to his care. He therefore exercises great authority in his diocese, and the people owe him the obedience they would give to Christ. But the task of a bishop in the mid-twentieth century is truly tremendous. Bishops realize that they cannot become personally acquainted with all the problems and situations which exist in the diocese. Yet they realize also that in order to make prudent and wise decisions, they must be in possession of the facts and have a true picture of the whole complex of life in their see. In order to have such a picture a bishop needs the help not only of his priests but also of the laity of his diocese.

In the ancient Church, the hierarchy was very much aware of the importance of keeping in close contact, working and even consulting with the people. St. Cyprian testifies to this spirit. "I have made it a rule ever since the beginning of my episcopate," he said, "to make no decision merely on the strength of my own personal opinion without consulting you [the priests and the deacons], without the approbation of the people."

In the early Church the whole Christian community took part in the election of bishops. The laity supplied information for councils and had a say in the formation of customs by which the whole Christian community lived.

Later centuries saw a decline in the participation of the laity in the life of the Church. Christian communities grew in size. During the period following the Peace of Constantine, the bishop came to be invested with authority even in secular matters. He became the defender of the people, the champion of their rights. He took on more and more the aspect of a secular as well as a religious ruler, especially since Church laws often became civil laws.

During the Dark Ages, when the Church was faced with the herculean task of civilizing the barbarians, even greater power and authority was centered in the bishop. In the absence of civil order and government, it was the bishop who established order in the cities. In medieval times, the authority of the hierarchy came to be stressed more and more, and the laity became a passive element. Even liturgically they did not participate in the life of the Church. Learning was the province of the clergy; any educated man was a cleric. The Protestant Reformation, which denied the sacramental priesthood altogether, occasioned a greater emphasis on the importance of hierarchy and clergy, while the passivity of the laity continued. With the establishment of seminaries, the clergy became better educated. The laity regarded the study of theology and any active role in the life of the Church as belonging exclusively to the clergy.

As immigration to America began, the dependence of the people on their priests increased. The masses of Catholics who left Europe to take up life in the New World were poor people of little education. They leaned heavily on the priests who came with them for leadership in every way. Consequently, they accepted what their priests said and did without question. They were content to supply the money, and they did a truly monumental job, as did their priests, of building and administration. The churches, schools, and other Catholic institutions which fill American cities are a tribute to these settlers. They preserved their own faith and made every provision for the preservation of the faith of their children. This is what they were called upon to do, and they did it magnificently.

The descendants of these immigrants are a different breed. They are no longer generally poor and uneducated; many of them are doctors, lawyers, and university professors. Those in the trades and service work have considerably more schooling and income than their immigrant ancestors. Catholic lay people are well informed, well educated, and well trained. They are leaders in their communities. Quite naturally, they do not have the same unquestioning attitude toward their priests which their ancestors had. They are adult in their relationship to the clergy. They are aware that they are mature, responsible members of the Church. They are eager to be articulate and active and to take their place in the whole life of the Church. This is not to say that they are anticlerical, but they are critical, as an adult is critical. They are not unquestioning; they are not content merely to be told what to do. They want to have a voice in what is being said and a part to play in what is being done. This situation prevails to a greater extent in some European countries as well.

For the first time in her history, the Church finds herself with a well-informed, enlightened laity, equipped to perform invaluable work and eager to play their full part in the life of the Church. The Pope, bishops, and priests are all aware of this. Some bishops have called upon their people to make known their wishes about the Vatican Council. Many priests realize that their people are partners with them in doing the work of the parish rather than merely executives of his commands. Usually when the bishop comes to dedicate a new church or school, he tells the people that this is their church, their school, built by them for the use of the whole Christian community.

Catholic lay people today feel that if the parish belongs to the people, they should have something to say about how it is run. The pastor represents the bishop, true, and he has pastoral authority; but the parish is a community, involving a real partnership between priest and people. Together they are to incarnate Christ in the neighborhood. Together they are to worship, learn, teach, grow in holiness, and work on the problems of the community. The parishioner who thinks that dropping his envelope into the basket on Sunday is all he ought to do as a member of the parish doesn't really understand the Church. Neither does the pastor who treats his parishioners literally as children, who doesn't consult them, seek their aid, encourage their initiative and zeal, learn from them, and respect their intelligence and judgment.

In his pastoral letter cited above, Cardinal Cushing brings out this point well and forcefully. After having pointed out that the layman, by reason of his very membership in the Church, must have a voice in the Church, Cardinal Cushing says that public opinion is necessary in the Church because of the nature of the Church itself:

The very structure of the Church further suggests that public opinion is an essential part of its existence as an institution. Since authority within the Church requires for its own effectiveness an almost day-to-day awareness of the state of Christian practice among its members, public opinion has a role to play here which cannot be abrogated or denied without at the same time placing in jeopardy the Christian life of the faithful and their efforts toward salvation. . . .

An informed public opinion provides the Church with . . . an actual account of the contemporary situation, a knowledge of the forces for good and evil which here and now confront Christians. A knowledge of this opinion makes possible intelligent appraisal and appropriate action for the guidance of the Christian conscience. Out of the living Church and its supernatural life come new applications of the truths of faith which in each generation are assimilated into that long tradition which is the history of the Church. . . . If a reading of the past teaches us anything, it demonstrates unmistakably that human ingenuity, under God's guidance, continually refreshes the Christian life, making possible ever new opportunities for greatness. Those revered heroes of the faith, raised to our altars as saints, were more often than not in times past just the ones guided by the Spirit into new and untried ways for the sake of the Kingdom. The alternative to this kind of change is stagnation and spiritual exhaustion. . . .

Public opinion within the church, nurtured and guided by religious teaching, brings to the world and its problems its own message of spiritual values and Christian hope. Nowhere have we better seen this apostolate at work than in the long series of social encyclicals which began almost one hundred years ago with Pope Leo XIII. Every level of Church authority must share with the Pontiff this care of souls which embraces all men. It is very far from being true to suppose that the beliefs of Catholics have an effect only on Catholics. Even as an institution the Church spreads its influence widely, and when an informed and apostolic public opinion exists within the Church, the whole world of necessity feels its force. . . .

Some temperaments among those in authority are inclined to narrow down the area of legitimate discussion, but this will have its own share of serious dangers. The formation of public opinion may be delayed by such action, but only for a short while. If it is long suppressed perilous frustrations will result, as well as an underground circulation of views which should have public discussion and exchange. Far better to tolerate some small indiscretion in the expression of public opinion than to discourage legitimate views and deprive the Church of that leaven which must invigorate the whole body.*

The Catholic who is religiously mature is well aware of his position within the Church. He is obedient to the Church not as a child is obedient—simply because he is forced to be—but with a commitment of his mind and heart, an obedience which is freely and intelligently given, an obedience which is a matter of love. The mature Catholic loves the Church not blindly but with full knowledge of her faults and shortcomings. He knows that the Church is imperfect in her human members and will continue to be imperfect until the end of the world.

In the face of the paradox of a divine but still imperfect Church, the religiously mature Catholic has a twofold attitude. On the one hand, he is eager to do what he can, as a responsible member of the Church, to make her more perfect. Hence his dedication to the apostolate of the Church, his desire to see the Church administered as well as possible, and his interest in the development of public opinion

* Cushing, *op. cit.*, pp. 13–16.

within the Church along open lines of communication among bishops, clergy, and laity. On the other hand, the religiously mature Catholic has great patience and a sense of humor. He needs both to avoid becoming bitter and cynical and just giving up. It is very frustrating for a zealous layman who knows the teachings and the directions of the popes on the lay apostolate and the liturgy to be told by his pastor, "We won't have any of that Catholic Action business around here," or to find no efforts made to have participation in the Mass. But true love for the Church and faith in the power of the Holy Spirit working within the Church will sustain the Catholic who really understands the Church, his place within her, and the real meaning and purpose of authority and obedience.

7

The Countless Disguises of Christ

In a discussion group one evening some years ago the question arose of just how a Christian was obliged to love his neighbor, meaning all the individuals who make up the crowds and groups in which one moves and of which one is a part in daily life. A member of the group replied that one must love these people as one loves a geographically remote people, say, the Ethiopians. The speaker's idea was that you wished no evil to the Ethiopians. You even felt a little sorry for them, inasmuch as at that time their country was being invaded by Italy. But when you came right down to it, you left the Ethiopians alone and they left you alone. You did no harm to them. You didn't kill them or steal from them or run off with their wives. You didn't lie to them or talk unkindly about them. In sum, you wished them well, which cost you no effort at all, for you were expected to do nothing for them. You never saw them or heard from them, but at least you had nothing against them.

Was this love, asked another member of the group? Was this even the barest minimum of love? Was this love in any conceivable sense of the word? Translated into terms of daily life, it meant that you didn't pick the pockets or intentionally step on the toes of people on a bus; you didn't say insulting things to people in the office or the shop. The trouble was that it was all a matter of *not* doing something to people. It was completely negative. Was love something negative? Oh, you had to go to the rescue of anyone in "extreme physical or spiritual danger," but short of that, it would be pretty much a matter of simply leaving people alone. Some members of the group could recall the definition of love which is given in philosophy—"to wish well to someone." What did it mean to wish well? Was it a purely academic, purely theoretical thing? Wasn't love a going out of oneself for the sake of another? Didn't it always involve some sort of giving of oneself? Didn't it always cost something? It costs nothing merely to wish someone well with the will. The priest and the Levite in the parable of the Good Samaritan wished the wounded man well, no doubt. They hoped that somehow he would recover. But they could hardly be said to have loved the stranger. Their well-wishing was ineffectual. The Samaritan's was effective. Therefore, his well-wishing was love.

It is often said that we must love everyone but that we do not have to like everyone. This distinction is made in order to emphasize that love is a matter of the will, not the feelings. Charity doesn't require that we get all gushy over people and have tender feelings about them. But at the same time, is it not possible that the distinction has been overdone? Has it perhaps promoted the impression that the love we call charity is a completely different kind of love from any other? It is different, of course, in the sense that it is supernatural, but should not that very fact make it a more perfect kind of love in every sense, even in the sense of total involvement of the person?

Feelings can be fickle things. They may or may not correspond to the constant, undeviating commitment of the will. The mother whose little boy has just tracked mud over her newly mopped kitchen floor could be pardoned for experiencing feelings which for a moment are mildly homicidal. So could the husband who hears a sound which tells him that his wife has once again backed the car into the side of the house. Yet in both cases there is genuine, unwavering love. It is quite possible to feel dislike or irritation or even disgust for someone for whom one actually has supernatural love. At the same time is the kind of person who says he dislikes people but practices charity toward them really loving his neighbor? Would not pity, compassion, sympathy, or some other genuine human feeling eventually show itself? Is it really possible to act with love when these sentiments are never present?

It is sometimes difficult to love. It is always difficult to be loved by one who is "practicing charity" on you. There is a vast difference between receiving a bowl of soup in a soup kitchen and being served a meal by the Little Brothers of the Poor. In the one instance you are merely a needy individual getting a bowl of soup. In the other you are presented with a bouquet of flowers and served beef Stroganoff and crepes suzette by someone who gives every indication that he is pleased at your presence. Perhaps the idea of what charity really is would be better defined if it were said that we must like our neighbor or at least try to like him if we are really to love him. Surely, anyone who is showing love for another human being must at least act as if he liked him. To show dislike of a person in the very act which is supposed to demonstrate love would be like giving with one hand and taking back with the other. It would be saying in action, "I'm loving you only because I have to in order to please God."

It has been said that the commandments define the outermost limits of love. The fifth commandment, then, sets the minimum requirements of love as far as physical welfare is concerned. One of the most elementary ways of showing love for another is to refrain from killing him or beating the daylights out of him. But this commandment refers to the spiritual welfare of one's neighbor, too. It forbids giving scandal and cooperating in the sin of another. The basis of this commandment, therefore, is the dignity and worth of the human person. Men's tremendous natural dignity is greatly enhanced by the fact that God has made them His own sons, has given them divine life, has imprinted Christ on them and dwells within them. The supernatural dignity of every human being—and in practice it applies to everyone, even the unbaptized and those in mortal sin, since all have been redeemed by Christ and destined to share God's life—gives a far more cogent reason for having love and reverence for all men. The minimum was expressed by the little boy who said to his companion, "If you weren't a temple of the Holy Ghost, I'd break your jaw." The maximum, the ideal—which should be the norm of every Christian—is shown by Christ. Jesus not only told the people that they were of much more worth than the grasses of the field and the birds of the air; He continually showed by His attitude and His actions that He knew that worth and that He truly loved men.

Christ could not bear to see anyone in pain or distress,

and often went to a great deal of trouble to help them. There are many instances in the Gospels which illustrate this point, but one is particularly striking. It occurs in the first chapter of St. Mark's Gospel, in the section which, probably alone of all the Gospels, gives us an account of a whole day in the life of Jesus. It was a Sabbath day. Christ had been teaching all day in the synagogue at Capharnaum. Leaving the synagogue, He went to the home of Peter, where He found Peter's mother-in-law sick in bed with a fever. Jesus cured her, and for once was rewarded quickly and tangibly—the old woman got up and served Him dinner. As soon as the sun was down, people began to come from all directions. As St. Mark says, "they brought to Him all who were ill and who were possessed. And the whole town had gathered together at the door" (Mk 1:32–33). How long it took Him to speak to each person who was afflicted and lay hands upon him is anybody's guess, but we may be sure that Jesus did not spare Himself the time and effort. Weary as Christ was after a long, hard day, He might have resorted to a mass cure. However, His understanding of human needs and His deep personal interest in each human being prompted Him to heal each individually.

Appreciation of the worth of a man should engender a great reverence for him as a person. This is a real reverence, showing itself in many ways; one way is the interest we take in others. We notice and give our attention to things of value. There are people who make you feel by the way they look at you and shake your hand that they consider you important, at least important enough to be worthy of a moment's undivided attention. There are others who make you wish you were invisible—who, for example, shake hands with you while looking at and talking to someone else, who walk up to someone to whom you are talking and, ignoring you, begin a conversation with him, who interrupt you, who ask a question and turn away without waiting for an answer, who are quite plainly not listening to a word you are saying. This rudeness derives from a lack of reverence for another person, a lack of charity. Contributing to the self-esteem of another can be very important at times. Some people need attention more than anything else. They need to be listened to, to be allowed to talk. All counselors are familiar with the person who comes for advice, talks on and on himself, and then, without the counselor's having opened his mouth, announces, "You have helped me very much."

Cana conferences have helped married couples greatly by bringing to their attention the different psychology of men and women. One of the aims of the meetings is to help husbands and wives understand one another's needs so that they may minister to each other and achieve a deeper spiritual union in their marriage. But this is a matter of charity, too. A husband who realizes that his wife needs to be told that he loves her, to be shown appreciation, to share his thoughts and problems will be more apt to talk to his wife and listen to her, to praise her cooking and housekeeping, to show affection and tenderness. A wife who realizes that her husband's greatest weakness is a tendency toward discouragement will be more apt to be sympathetic, understanding, and above all loyal and encouraging.

But an understanding of the different psychology of men

and women can be a great help in showing love for others in all other human relationships as well. The man who realizes that little things mean a lot to a woman, that women are more interested in people than in things, that they notice details which might escape a man, and that they are more sensitive and more subjective in their approach to human relationships is apt to be more considerate of the feelings of all the women with whom he comes in contact in daily life. Keeping the psychology of the other person in mind is extremely important in loving others. It is easy to hurt a child by brushing him off and refusing to listen to him, as if he had no valid thoughts or feelings. When an adult realizes that children have their own way of thinking and expressing themselves he will be more apt to treat them with the patience and interest which spring from love. Knowledge of the psychology of other persons also means having respect for the other person's needs as a thinking human being. Reverence for another as a person requires that we allow others not only to talk but also to express their opinions, even when those opinions differ from ours. A truly charitable person even tries to see the other fellow's point as far as possible. If he disagrees, he does not make the other feel like a fool for holding the differing opinion. He actively tries to shield others from embarrassment and shame.

Once again, it is Christ Who gives the example. His conversation with the Samaritan woman at Jacob's Well is a masterpiece of gentleness and charity. It could be taken as a lesson in tact, diplomacy, psychology, good manners—any number of virtues. Certainly, above all, it is a lesson in reverence and love.

The story, as told in the fourth chapter of St. John's Gospel, is a familiar one. Jesus and His apostles were in Samaria. They paused at the famous landmark known as Jacob's Well. There Jesus declared that He would rest, sitting at the side of the well, while the apostles went into town to buy food. A Samaritan woman approached, carrying a water jar on her head. She ignored the Jewish man who was sitting there on the side of the well, for two reasons. First of all, a mere woman would not presume to speak to a man; it would be beneath his dignity to pretend to notice her. Second, she was a Samaritan, someone whom a Jew would despise.

The woman went quietly about her business, preparing to lower her jar into the well, when suddenly she was startled to hear this man speak to her. He, a man and a Jew, was asking a favor of her, putting Himself in her debt, as it were. He was asking for a drink of water. The woman expressed her astonishment that a Jew would speak to a Samaritan woman and ask a favor of her. Jesus replied, "If thou didst know the gift of God, and who it is who says to thee, 'Give me to drink,' thou, perhaps, wouldst have asked of him, and he would have given thee living water."

The woman was intrigued now. Jesus wanted her to be. His intention was to save her. He wanted to give her the gift of faith. He led her gently to the point where she wanted this mysterious and wonderful water He was talking about. She arrived at the point, and asked for it.

Now came a delicate moment. Jesus had to enter into the painful matter of the woman's sinful life, which constituted an obstacle to her acceptance of faith. He said simply, "Go, call thy husband and come here." The woman replied that she had no husband. Now Jesus had to be blunt. Yet He managed to soften the confrontation with guilt somewhat by giving the woman credit for telling the truth. "Thou hast said well, 'I have no husband,' for thou hast had five husbands, and he whom thou now hast is not thy husband. In this thou hast spoken truly."

The woman was ashamed. She abruptly changed the subject and brought up a religious question about where God was to be worshiped. Jesus did not say, "Just a moment, woman. Don't try to change the subject." He had succeeded in getting the woman to look at her life, even if very briefly; He would not embarrass her further. He went along with her and replied to her question, explaining very patiently and kindly the true meaning of worship. Finally, He openly told the woman who He was in order that she might accept Him and be saved.

This is one of many incidents in which the Gospels abound showing the regard Jesus had for people's feelings. His attitude was the farthest possible remove from the concept of "love as you love the Ethiopians."

All Catholics know that the fifth commandment specifically forbids hatred—wishing evil to or seeking to do evil to another—any anything which would harm one's neighbor, such as scandal. Put in such general terms, the fifth commandment does not seem to make very great demands on us. Applied to the concrete circumstances of everyday life, however, it becomes tremendously challenging. No modern Christian, for example, can avoid coming to grips with the problem of racial and religious prejudice.

No discussion of Christian love could possibly be held without facing up to this issue, which, more than any other social problem of our time, puts the depth and maturity of our charity to the test our Lord devised: "By this will all men know that you are my disciples, if you have love for one another." In this, above all, it is important to go well beyond the minimal demands of charity. Not that these are always being met, by any means—there are plenty of cases of necessity which arise from bad housing and other social conditions that minimal charity would rectify. But the constant insult to human dignity which is offered in many ways, day after day, is not recognized widely enough as being incompatible with Christlike charity. White people who say, "Let the Negroes have their own neighborhoods and schools and whatever else they want, but we don't want to mix with them and they don't want to mix with us," show a profound ignorance of what Negroes think and feel. The cruelest feature of segregation is the insult it offers by saying, "You are in your very essence inferior to me. You are subhuman."

It is astonishing how naive people can be on this subject. Some years ago, in a talk at which both Negroes and whites were present, a priest declared very dogmatically that Negroes themselves wanted segregation. He quoted the old canard, "Birds of a feather flock together." He cited as proof the fact that Negroes weren't demanding to be admitted to certain restaurants. He went on and on, serenely unconscious of the fact that what he was saying bore no relationship to the facts. Another priest cut in. "Father," he said, "there are a lot of Negroes here. Do you mind taking a poll, just to see whether they agree with what you are saying?" Every single Negro present declared that he was completely opposed to segregation. Many added that they resented very much being barred from certain restaurants but kept away because they did not like the unpleasantness of being told they would not be served.

Nowadays, when more and more Negroes are demanding their rights, it is harder to close the mind to the facts, but an astonishing number of people still say, "These are only the troublemakers. The decent Negro doesn't feel this way." This is the same as saying that the decent Negro is not a human being with the feelings and sensibilities which all human beings have. A human being doesn't really mind being told that he can't belong to a certain organization or live in a certain neighborhood because of some extrinsic circumstance which is not a reflection on himself. A man may be disappointed at not being able to build in a certain subdivision because he can't afford to put up the kind of house which will meet the requirements, but he will not be wounded in his person. But this is different from being barred from a neighborhood because of the color of one's skin. A man in this position realizes that he is being told he is inferior to others because of his color. He is being told that no matter how much money he has, how much intelligence, how much education, how much culture, or how much character or even sanctity, he is somehow inferior in his very person to others and therefore not worthy to live among them. This is what makes segregation incompatible with Christian charity. It is founded on an idea which is a contradiction of Christian belief. It is a continual rejection of a human person, not for a fault, not for something he can change, but because of a prejudice which prevents him from being treated according to his dignity as a man and as a son of God. A Catholic who holds that human beings are not equally endowed with dignity as persons and as children of God is guilty of a sin against faith itself.

Many problems complicate the issue of segregation. For example, there is the moral principle that charity does not bind short of extreme necessity, where a serious hardship is involved. But if the early Christians had exhibited such a minimal and legalistic brand of charity, would Christianity have even gotten off the ground? Is anything less than a charity which is truly Christlike worthy of a Christian today?

Many good people agree that the racial question is a great challenge to Christians today but are honestly at a loss to know what they can do personally about the situation. A group of Catholic couples in a small town in the Far West had this problem; not a single Negro lived in their town. What they did was to get hold of some Negro newspapers and magazines in order to gain a better understanding of the Negroes' problems and their reactions to discrimination. They made it a point to write encouraging letters to political leaders, editors, and others who stood up for interracial justice. Some Catholics, living in all-white neighborhoods of cities where there is a large Negro population, attend local meetings of the National Association for the Advancement of Colored People. Others have invited a single Negro or a couple to their homes, not to discuss race but simply to become better acquainted. One Holy Name Society in an all-white parish invited a Negro psychologist to speak at one of their meetings. These are little things, to be sure, but they help people become active and involved in an issue which must be the concern of every Christian.

It is significent that when Christ was asked to describe

what it means to love one's neighbor, He answered by giving the parable of the Good Samaritan, which has a religious as well as a racial aspect. The Samaritans, as we indicated above, were not only a different tribe from the Jews but they also had a different religion, one which the Jews loathed as a mixture of Judaism and paganism. Religious prejudice still shows itself today toward a people who have suffered tremendously because of their "race" as well: the Jews. People will often deny that they have anything against Jews, but the clubs to which they belong and the summer resorts where they spend their vacations are very likely to have a policy of admitting Gentiles only. Some say that they dislike Jews because of personality traits which they find unattractive and irritating. Any person who is truly mature should see this as an illogical generalization. It is as unjust and uncharitable to say that all Jews are aggressive and unethical in business as it is to say that all Irishmen are drunkards and brawlers.

In reality, when Jews are discriminated against, it is really because of their religion; after all, that and that alone is what makes a Jew a Jew. The senselessness of such discrimination was brought into focus by Groucho Marx when his children were barred from a swimming pool which was for Gentiles only. Groucho called and explained that his children were only half Jewish inasmuch as their mother was a Gentile. "Would it be all right," he asked "if they went in up to the waist?" Some Christians in past ages have persecuted Jews for religious reasons, attempting to justify their behavior on the grounds that the Jews crucified Christ. No one who lays any claim to religious maturity or even common sense would be guilty of such thinking, which is both utterly unreasonable and utterly un-Christian.

The Parable of the Good Samaritan has added meaning today, when the division among Christians is coming more and more to be recognized for the scandal that it is. Christians are becoming increasingly aware of the fact that even though they are separated brethren, they are brethren. On all sides the realization is growing that while there are real and important doctrinal differences, there is also a great bond which unites all who profess to follow Jesus Christ—the bond of love. While they agree quite frankly to disagree, Christians can work together with one another and with Jews and those of other faiths in a spirit of love. This love should be more than a matter of words uttered at patriotic rallies and social get-togethers; like all love, it should be practical and effective. Its first manifestation perhaps should be to do others the courtesy of granting that they are sincere in their beliefs. This is not religious indifferentism or anything like it. It is simply a matter of charity. Its opposite—and this is surely a matter of rash and uncharitable judgment—was given expression by a Catholic who was watching an evangelist on television: "Look at that faker up there."

Love for those whom we call our separated brethren should manifest itself also in an attempt to know something about them and about what they believe. A priest was startled one afternoon by a voice over the telephone demanding to know, "What is a Baptist?" As the priest was catching his breath and trying to figure out how to formulate an answer, the agitated voice continued, "I went to a wake last night. The people were Baptists. There was no crucifix over the casket. There was no kneeler there. Nobody knelt down to say a prayer, and nobody was holding a rosary. What kind of religion is this? Don't Baptists believe in God?" One can easily imagine the counterpart to this: "Reverend, I went to a Catholic wake. There was a big crucifix above the casket. Everybody who came in went up to the casket and knelt down and prayed. Do these people bow down before graven images? Do they worship the dead?"

An adult American Catholic who is just now realizing that there is such a thing as a Baptist is surely displaying an amazing lack of interest in his Protestant neighbors. And anyone who would conclude that the absence of such articles as rosary beads and crucifixes bespeaks disbelief in God betrays that fact that he knows nothing about the beliefs and practices of millions of sincere Christians who call themselves Protestants. It is often said that what people outside the Church know of her is not the Church at all but a wildly distorted caricature. Protestants might claim the same thing as regards the ideas which many Catholics have of what Protestants believe.

Charity requires that men discard both their prejudices and their ignorance, and excellent means to this end are friendly discussions—a Catholic woman and her Baptist friend quietly explaining to each other, over coffee in the kitchen, what they believe, not with the idea of changing each other's minds but simply with the idea of helping each other toward greater sympathy for and understanding of others. Many opportunities are at hand nowadays both for dialogue among Catholics, Protestants, and Jews and for meetings which help people discover what their various faiths have in common as well as in what they differ. One public high school uses its social studies course each year as a means of informing the students on these subjects.

As a priest who was asked to address a Presbyterian young people's club mounted the platform and looked out over the audience, he could read in many eyes questions about Purgatory, indulgences, worship of Mary. He began by stating that Catholics and Presbyterians had a great deal in common. Then he launched into a talk on the Blessed Trinity, not making an issue of whether those in the audience believed the doctrine but simply presenting Catholic teaching on the Trinity. The atmosphere changed completely. The listeners were genuinely interested. They asked much the same sort of questions a group of Catholic young people might have asked. Then, finally, a few questions were asked about Mary and confession and the other expected subjects, but they were put forward in a spirit of genuine inquiry, and the audience was receptive to the explanations which were given.

There was a time not long ago when Protestants in the United States were undisputed masters of the scene. Sometimes real bigotry, a real lack of Christian charity, was displayed toward Catholics, who were often regarded as un-American and addicted to all sorts of superstitions. Today, although Catholics are still a minority, the picture has changed. It is no longer deemed necessary to be a Protestant in order to be a "real American," and Catholics are no longer looked down upon except in some rural areas in the South. Name-calling is not so common as it used to be. But there is a more subtle form of uncharitableness; and it comes from Catholics. It is epitomized by the remark of an ex-Catholic when he was asked whether he had become a

Protestant. "I lost my faith," he replied, "not my mind." It manifests itself in a rather pitying condescension: "The poor Protestants. They really have nothing. We have the Pope and the sacraments and the Mass and all the teachings of Jesus Christ. They have only the Bible, and there is no one to tell them what it means."

Lack of charity between Protestants and Catholics has manifested itself in different ways. Protestant intolerance of Catholics usually takes the form of verbal attack. Catholics display uncharitableness by simply refusing to take Protestants seriously as religious people; when they show interest, it is usually in terms of convert work. You might make a Catholic out of a Protestant, they indicate, but you couldn't learn anything from him as a Protestant. Recently, with the blossoming of the ecumenical movement and the wonderful spirit of Christian brotherhood which Pope John XXIII showed, more Catholics are taking an interest in Protestants, and they are finding that this works to their own advantage also. To cite an example, there has been a good deal of cooperation and communication between Lutherans and Catholics in Germany. The Lutherans have profited by seeing Catholic sacramental and liturgical life, while the Catholics have profited by seeing the Lutheran veneration of the Scriptures. Protestants are coming to realize that some of the things to which they objected are not really part of the Church's life and teachings. Catholics are seeing that some of the demands of the Reformers were quite justified and have actually been or are being taken into consideration by the Church.

It is of great importance that Catholics, Protestants, and Jews work together on various civic and social projects, both for the sake of the work itself and also because it establishes a common bond of friendship, understanding, and love. Such cooperation is to be found today in organizations like the National Council of Christians and Jews and the National Council on Religion and Race. The latter is doing a truly remarkable job in bringing Catholics, Protestants, and Jews together on matters which lie heavily on the consciences of all. Groups and movements like these cannot help but foster a spirit of understanding and love among men who call God Father.

God has told us that we must love our neighbor as we love ourself. Keeping this precept in mind doesn't make it easier to love others, perhaps, but it does make it easier to understand how we are to love others. How do I love myself? Well, first of all, I not only love myself; I like myself. I know my faults and I dislike them, but disliking my faults doesn't cause me to dislike myself. I expect others to understand and be patient with me. They should know that I am irritable in the morning and that certain things rub me the wrong way. They should realize that I have the sort of temperament I have, and make allowances for it. When I say foolish things or act in a ridiculous manner they should make light of it, realizing as I do that this is not the real me. They should be aware, as I am at all times, that despite my very real faults and unattractive character defects, despite my pride and my selfishness and my thoughtlessness, deep down inside I am a pretty wonderful person.

This is what the Lord expects us to do and feel for others.

8

SANCTITY AND SEX

A priest who conducts a course in marriage for the seniors at a Catholic high school for boys makes it a practice of giving the class a questionnaire at the beginning of the course each year. One of the questions he asks is, "Where did you receive the information you have about sex?" Year after year it is the same story. The replies reveal that a few have been given "birds and bees" talks by their father or mother. Some have received information from a priest; a few more have read marriage manuals or books on the facts of life. The vast majority—a good 90 percent—have learned what they know from the streets. It is not surprising, therefore, that they have a negative, immature, and sometimes distorted idea of sex.

These Catholic young men are very aware of the force of the sexual urge. They are aware, too, that they are forbidden to indulge this strong urge. But they do not understand why. In their minds it is simply a matter of a law. If you were to ask them why any premarital use of sex is wrong, they would reply, "It is against the sixth commandment." True, of course, but utterly negative, incomplete, and unsatisfactory. A person with such a negative idea of chastity could never understand sex, love, and marriage. He would be unaware of the Christian concept of sex. The practice of chastity, always difficult for a young man, would be rendered much more difficult for him. Much of the beauty and meaning of life would be lost on him, for a real appreciation of the full meaning of sex is necessary for a true understanding of human nature and of life itself.

It is astonishing how few people fully appreciate the meaning of sex. The negative view of the high-school students just described is shared by a great many grown men and women, both married and single. Much of the blame for this state of affairs must be laid to parents, but some priests, nuns, and religious educators also come in for a share.

The parent who has a negative attitude toward sex is bound to transmit it to his child; he is incapable of giving the child a positive idea. Any questions about sex are apt to be met with embarrassment: "We don't talk about things like that." No sex education is given, much less a Christian one. Despite all the talk about how important it is, few parents give their children sex instruction. The upshot is that many and perhaps most children learn about the meaning of sex from a source which is, to say the least, unsatisfactory. At best it might be a book which is scientifically accurate but pagan and animalistic in tone; more often it is another child whose information is 10 percent biological fact and 90 percent misinformation, and who will convey the whole message in a sniggering, indecent, conspiratorial way, using all the four-letter words. Thus the impression is given—and often enough it is never entirely eradicated afterwards—that the whole business of sex is shameful.

Nuns and priests are much more aware today of the importance of giving young people a full Christian explanation of sex, as are many parents. But there is all too often still a hangover from the older books and methods. We say, of course, that sex itself is not evil, but we then proceed to explain chastity in terms of not doing things. We do have to teach what is sinful in this matter as in any other (although it does seem that a great deal more time and effort is devoted to teaching what is sinful here than in other areas of morality, some of which are more serious), but the manner of presentation need not and should not be negative.

A case in point is the way questions about the morality of necking and petting are often answered. An adolescent asks whether these actions are sinful. Usually the first answer is, "Yes." Then the explanation is added, "These things are sinful for you because you are not married. They are all right for married people." Rarely is the really correct answer given —that these actions are good and holy, not just "all right" for married people but an important part of that act by which they give themselves to one another as God's partners in the sacrament of marriage. After this initial answer it could easily be shown why such actions would be wrong for an unmarried person.

What is the difference? It is in the impression given, on the one hand, that the use of sex is wrong in itself but is rendered acceptable by marriage, and on the other, that the use of sex is a good and holy thing and that it is only its misuse which is wrong. It is very difficult for a healthy young man to feel that what he has so strong an urge to do and what is so natural and instinctive is wrong and sinful;

it is not so difficult for him to understand that it would be wrong for him to perform what is in itself a good and natural act because he has no right to do so here and now. A girl who has been taught that this is something wicked and sinful and shameful will also find it hard to feel, now that she is wearing a wedding ring, that all of a sudden it is perfectly all right.

In order really to practice the virtue of chastity one must have a true appreciation of the meaning of sex. A negative or erroneous idea will not do. Sex is a very important part of human nature. It must be seen in its full context, as part of the mystery of the human person.

Man is unique. Like animals, he eats and sleeps; like God, he knows and loves. Unlike anything else in Heaven or on earth, he laughs. And unlike anything else in Heaven or on earth, he makes love. God loves; animals mate; only man *makes love*. This is the key to understanding the mystery of sex. Sex is deeply and uniquely human; it goes to the very roots of a human being. God is pure spirit; therefore, He loves as pure spirit. Man is a composite of spirit and matter; therefore, he expresses himself through his body. He expresses worship for God through words, posture, and movements and thoughts by words, gestures and facial expressions. He expresses love, too, through his body, by a hand clasp, an embrace, a kiss, a look of affection. And that deepest of all human love, love between man and woman, he expresses by the deepest involvement of the body, sexual union.

The Kinsey reports on sexual behavior have been criticized in various ways. Perhaps the most serious criticism which can be leveled at them is that they give the impression that sex in human beings is a purely physiological function. There is much talk of "outlets," and no talk at all of love. Yet to separate human sex from love is to rob it of its significance. It is to make it a merely material and therefore shallow and superficial thing instead of the deeply mysterious and beautiful thing it is, the means by which two persons are united in the entirety of their bodies and souls, the means by which they give themselves to one another in love.

The word *love* is bandied about a great deal. Like other fundamental things, it is hard to define. Philosophical definitions seem too cold and sterile. It is more satisfactory to describe love than to try to define it. One of the characteristics of love is that it involves the giving of gifts. We give to those we love. We give time that we might begrudge to a stranger or a mere acquaintance. We give presents to those we love as a sign of our love; the more we love the more expensive the present is apt to be. This is so because giving the present is really a gift of oneself, as is one's gift of time, attention, help, and company. This fact was well appreciated by a young lady who proudly exhibited an engagement ring which her fiancé had just given her on her birthday. "Why, that cheapskate!" one of the men in the office exclaimed. "He gives you an engagement ring on your birthday so he doesn't have to buy you a birthday present." The girl only smiled more broadly. "I thought of that," she said, "but it doesn't make any difference. This ring is a promise that he is going to give me himself, and that is what really counts."

The mystery of sex is the mystery of the human person. Why is it that what is merely a physiological function in animals is such a profound and significant thing in human beings? It is because sex in humans is all tied up with the self, the personality, and thus with the giving of oneself in love to another. In some mysterious way the sexual faculty is the most personal part of us—of our person. Everyone senses this. The very words *personal, private,* and *intimate* that are applied to the sexual faculty are proof of it. And this faculty, alone among all that we possess, is not designed for our own use. We possess it not for ourselves but in order that we may give ourselves to another. And this gift of oneself, so complete and total, is by its very nature a unique and lifelong giving of self. It is a union not merely of bodies but of persons, a union of souls which is achieved through this most complete and intimate bodily union.

The sixth commandment, which concerns the proper use of sex, mentions only the sin of adultery. Everyone knows, of course, that this commandment forbids not only adultery but any illicit use of sex. The mention of adultery, however, makes explicit the essential connection between sex and marriage. Only in marriage may sex be used, and then only in accordance with its purpose. Any sexual act is forbidden to unmarried persons. This wonderful faculty may not be used lightly; it may only be given as a gift of self for life to the person with whom one has exchanged marriage vows.

Some see this precept as only a grudging toleration of sex. The Church, they say, does not really approve of the whole thing. She restricts the use of sex as far as she possibly can, and takes all the joy and spontaneity out of it. Actually, the reverse is the case. Sex, like anything else, is a part of human life and must be seen and used in that context. Only then does it have its full meaning and beauty. Not the Church but the advocates of the extramarital use of sex are the real enemies of sex. They make it a matter of pleasure only, or self-expression or experience or release, instead of a matter of love which deeply involves the whole person. They rob sex of its significance and make it shallow and strangely disappointing. The promiscuous person must confess in moments of complete honesty that he wonders what all the shouting is about. The anticipation of great satisfaction is usually there, to be sure, but not the fulfillment. The trouble is that once sex is divorced from love and put on an animal plane, the person defeats himself. Sexual hunger comes from the soul, not from the body only. It is the need to love and be loved which is trying to express itself. Sex can succeed in satisfying this hunger only when it is part of the total gift of self which marriage involves.

The expression "to make love" says more than might be immediately evident. A man and woman must build their love. They must water it and nourish it. If sex is merely a matter of obtaining pleasure from one another, love will never develop. Conjugal love entails a giving of oneself in hundreds of ways. A man who doesn't talk to his wife will be an unsatisfactory lover. A wife who is not interested in pleasing her husband with her cooking and her other wifely duties will hardly be really pleasing to him in her most intimate wifely role. This was very well summed up by a Catholic doctor in the answer he gave to a high-school boy. The boy had asked, "How long does it take to have marriage relations?" The doctor hesitated for a moment, then replied, "If you are trying to get something—a few minutes; if you are trying to give something—a lifetime."

Negativism can take the beauty out of everything. Nowhere does it do a more complete job than in sex; nowhere are the thou-shalt-nots more frustrating. What is needed is less talk about the sins into which one is forever apt to fall and more talk about the virtue of chastity. Too many Catholics are obsessed with the fear of sinning against the sixth and ninth commandments. No confession of theirs is complete without the mention of that specifically Catholic sin, impure thoughts, which in most cases turn out to have been indeliberate. So much attention is given to the ease with which one can fail to be chaste in thought, word, or action that not nearly enough is paid to chastity itself. According to the norm of "I am chaste if I don't do this and I don't do that," the best way to practice chastity would be to have a paralytic stroke.

Of course, one is keeping the sixth and ninth commandments if one resists temptations to impure thoughts, words, and actions. These commandments forbid us to give in to these things. But is one who merely resists temptation really practicing chastity? It is often said that chastity is an intensely positive virtue, and almost as often, unfortunately, these are just words. To practice this virtue which is so basic to the Christian life, one must understand what it is and what it entails.

Chastity is that virtue which regulates the use of sex. But how is sex to be used? It is not really satisfactory to say that it is to be used by married people and that it is not to be used at all by the unmarried. Actually, married people often practice chastity by refraining from the use of their marriage rights, and even for the unmarried the practice of chastity does not mean simply a nonuse of sex. It is impossible, really, not to use sex. This does not mean, of course, that it is impossible to refrain from sexual relations. But sex means more than the marriage act itself. It includes all the endowments of personality which are involved in masculinity and femininity. Any man, married or single, is using his gift of sex when he acts in a fatherly way or does anything which is associated with manliness. Any woman, be she wife, unmarried woman, or nun, is using her gift of sex when she gives herself as only a woman can, in the service of others.

A young married man with a somewhat anticlerical streak once asked a boyhood friend who had become a priest, "What do priests do all day?" "I'll tell you what I do," the priest replied. "I get up in the morning. I go over to the church and say Mass. I come back to the rectory and have breakfast. Then I go up to my room and sit down and practice celibacy all day. Try it sometime!" This was effective as a retort, but it did not really answer the question. It is presumed that the priest practiced chastity as well as celibacy. But he did not practice chastity by sitting in his room all day, off in an ivory tower, away from the people who call him Father. He practiced chastity by using the powers of his manhood in the priestly work to which God had called him. He practiced chastity by being, in every sense, a spiritual father.

Chastity is sometimes referred to as the angelic virtue. This is an absurdity which comes from confusing chastity with purity, a much wider concept. Chastity is a specifically human and particularly humanizing virtue. It doesn't make us like the angels; it makes us fully men and women. It is the proper exercise of manhood and womanhood, a virtue which is utterly necessary for the living of the Christian life. Therefore, it should mark every Christian, married or single, religious or lay, though its practice will vary according to the state of life in which each Christian lives and works within the Mystical Body of Christ.

A married couple practices chastity by giving themselves to one another in that unique union which is marital love. But this giving of self in love, always good in any lawful marriage, takes on much greater meaning when the lovers are Christians. Their union is a sacramental union. The gifts which they give to each other in love are actually Christ's. All that has been said of sex as a good and uniquely human thing is tremendously heightened by the fact of Baptism and incorporation into Christ. The human body, good in its natural state, becomes Christ's body, because the Christian is grafted onto Christ by Baptism; it becomes the tabernacle in which dwells the Blessed Trinity itself. This great fact has never found better expression than in St. Paul's words:

> Now the body is not for immorality, but for the Lord, and the Lord for the body. Now God has raised up the Lord and will also raise us up by his power. Do you not know that your bodies are members of Christ? Shall I then take the members of Christ and make them members of a harlot? By no means! Or do you not know that he who cleaves to a harlot becomes one body with her? "For the two," it says, "shall be in one flesh." But he who cleaves to the Lord is one spirit with him. Flee immorality. Every sin that a man commits is outside the body, but the immoral man sins against his own body. Or do you not know that your members are the temple of the Holy Spirit, who is in you, whom you have from God, and that you are not your own? For you have been bought at a great price. Glorify God and bear him in your body. [1 Cor 6:13–20]

The great gift which a Christian man and wife give each other is an increase in the divine life, the life of Jesus Christ. This they give to each other as they exchange vows at the altar, and they continue to share this gift through their expression of love, since that expression is part of Christ's sacrament. Their lovemaking is therefore sacred, the exercise of a supernatural virtue. The virtue of chastity prompts Christian husbands and wives to give themselves to one another in a specifically Christian way, with the reverence a Christian brings to use of sex. Here again, the pagan might complain that the Christian attitude is antisex and opposed to the free, unfettered use he favors. But actually, the Christian attitude of reverence gives sex a deeper meaning, making it not only holier but also more human, as we have said. This thought was expressed even in Old Testament times. The angel Raphael told the young Tobias why it was that his wife's previous husbands had been destroyed by a demon on their wedding night: "For they who in such manner receive matrimony, as to shut out God from themselves and from their mind, and to give themselves to their lust, as the horse or mule which have not understanding, over them the devil hath power" (Tob 6:17). Tobias heeded the advice of the angel. He reminded his bride, "For we are the children of saints, and we must not be joined together like the heathens that know not God" (Tob 8:5). The falsity of the pagan position is demonstrated again and again by couples in the Christian Family Movement and in Cana conferences. Many of them have stated that as their spiritual life deepened, their Christian awareness grew, and their understanding of Christian married love increased, their sexual union became a source of greater joy, happiness, and fulfillment in every sense.

Chastity, like every other virtue, is related to charity. Married couples practice chastity in all aspects of relationship to one another. St. Paul says that husbands must love their wives as Christ loves the Church and as they love their own bodies. Christ's love for the Church is self-sacrificial; so is that of the truly chaste husband. He might with perfect justice insist on his marriage rights at a time when his wife is tired or disinclined to make love, but chastity as well as charity would prompt him to make a sacrifice out of consideration for her.

Sometimes chastity calls for downright heroism from married people, a heroism which is not even suspected by many who are unmarried. How many couples are practicing chastity to a heroic degree by abstaining from expressing their love for long periods of time? We refer not to those who "make love by a calendar" because they want a second car or a new patio behind their split level but to those who are laboring under real economic hardship or who have a serious problem of health. In one such case the wife had had an operation for cancer. The doctor warned the couple that pregnancy might well activate the malignant growth. The husband told a priest, "I have no choice. I love this woman. I will not do anything to harm her." He had faith enough to realize that to practice contraception would hurt his wife spiritually. To forego the full expression of marital love for the sake of luxuries is simply to prefer a lesser good to a greater; to forego it for the sake of love itself is a great expression of chastity.

One of the services which the Cana movement has rendered, as we said above, is to make people more aware of the psychological characteristics which are a part of sex. An understanding of these characteristics is necessary for a successful marriage. Man and wife must know each other's strengths and weaknesses in order to understand each other's needs. Each must know his own in order to be able to fulfill his role in marriage and in the family. A husband must be aware of his strengths—his masculine drive, his fortitude, his objectivity, his logical approach to truth, and all the other characteristics of manhood—in order to use it to be the head of his wife. He must realize, too, his weakness, the weakness of man, the builder and doer—a tendency toward discouragement—in order to seek from his wife the inspiration and encouragement which it is her part to give. He must also know his wife's greatest need, the need to be wanted and appreciated, the need for affection and love. He must know the value which women put on things which seem unimportant to a man, and understand that a woman needs to be told she is loved and appreciated in hundreds of different little ways.

Chastity in marriage requires that husband and wife give to each other and receive from each other in the wholeness of their persons. Love which finds its consummation in the marital act shows itself in such little things as the sacrifice of a favorite television program or praise for a well-cooked meal. One husband in a premarriage talk to a group of young men described what it means to be a lover. The young men were thinking of the fire-breathing lovers they had seen in the movies. This young husband was much more realistic. "I find that my wife is more apt to become tender and affectionate," he said, "when I say something like, 'Honey, you've been working hard all day. Why don't you go on in and sit down, and let me do the dishes?' "

Chastity in marriage has the effect of broadening the married couple. It opens them up, gives them understanding and warmth, and widens the borders of their love. Paradoxically, their love for one another leads them to love others. A man and wife whose love continues to be centered exclusively upon one another, like a couple on a perpetual honeymoon, find that their love does not mature. Childless couples face this danger. Nature itself seeks to help married love mature through parenthood. But the borders of love should extend even beyond the family to the neighborhood, the community, the world. Once again the Christian Family Movement has proved an important point: while a couple grow as Christians by working in the apostolate of the Church, the wider interests they develop have a deepening effect upon their family life and their conjugal love.

Among the unmarried chastity is all too often thought to be negative, a question of avoiding the use of sex. But as we said, it is impossible not to use sex, in the sense that the psychological characteristics of sex are part of the personality. A sexless being, one which did not exhibit qualities of manliness or womanliness, would be an inhuman creature, more like a machine than a person. One such, a tight-lipped, vinegary mother superior, was aptly described by her pastor as a "supervirgin." Virgin she was, but without the warmth and humanity and womanliness which comes from true chastity.

Married people, too, can be like this. One middle-aged wife complained to her pastor, "Here we are in our fifties, and that husband of mine still wants to make love. I told him we were too old for that sort of foolishness. What is he, Father, an animal?" The woman was shocked at the priest's reply. "No, your husband is not an animal. He is a man. And that is something you would not understand, because you are not much of a woman."

The vast majority of young unmarried persons should see

the type of chastity they practice as a preparation for their future role in marriage. All too often they are not aware that God is preparing them for a real vocation within the Mystical Body. Just as a priest prepares for his vocation in a seminary, just as a religious prepares in the novitiate, these young people are truly preparing for their vocation—marriage. In and through that state of life they will do the work Christ has in store for them and will become sanctified and made ready for their eternal destiny.

Too many modern teen-agers regard dating as simply recreation, a means of fun and pleasure. This is certainly not the attitude of the Church, which regards dating in general as a remote preparation for marriage and engagement company-keeping as a proximate preparation. This is not to say that the Church lacks cheerfulness and humor and seeks to rob young people of the fun they should normally have while growing up, but she is opposed to irresponsibility. Boys and girls should associate with one another; they will never develop a mature attitude toward sex or come to understand the opposite sex if they do not.

Moreover, in the crucial years of the teens a boy needs the influence of a girl and, more subtly but nonetheless truly, a girl needs the influence of a boy. Adolescents have a deep need for understanding, inspiration, and affection, and it is a well-known fact that they often find it difficult to open up with older people, to show their feelings or accept affecton. Many a boy, during this period, is helped immeasurably by a girl, and vice versa. This is a sort of foretaste of the mutual help which husbands and wives give to each other in marriage, the man giving affection and appreciation, the woman giving encouragement and inspiration. The chaste boy or girl can give help to another which will have good effects for a whole lifetime. All priests are familiar with the case of a boy who comes back to confession for the first time in several years and gives as an explanation, "Father, I met a wonderful girl, and she has made me want to be a better Catholic."

A positive approach to chastity is necessary for Catholic young people. Simply telling them that any actions which arouse passion are sinful is not enough. The whole concept of chastity should be impressed upon them—not a prohibition to use sex but an encouragement to use their youthful manliness and womanliness to help others, those they are dating in particular. In season and out of season Catholic youths (in fact, all Catholics) need to be reminded that we are not the same as those who do not believe as we do. Youths need ideals; youths need a challenge. What higher ideal is there than Christ? What greater inspiration can there be than the realization that we are members of Christ's Body and temples of the Holy Spirit? What greater challenge is there than that of living a life which is in accordance with the supernatural truths which we believe?

The cry of youth is the same old human cry: "But everybody's doing it." Any Catholic who is even beginning to strive for maturity has to face up to the fact that he is not "everybody," that he is a child of God with the standards and ideals of the children of God. Is this too much to expect from Catholic youth? The only answer is that it is what God expects. The Church must hold up the ideal and provide the means of living up to it, which she does. Certainly, there is nothing to be lost in presenting to Catholic youth the full meaning of chastity, stressing its relation to charity and its positive aspect. Would not anything less be a betrayal of them? Later on, in marriage, they will have to live lives of chastity as it is lived in the married state; before marriage they must know that love expresses itself here and now in helping the other person preserve chastity and remain in God's grace. Confessors know that one of the strongest motives which can be given to young people for not engaging in necking and petting is the motive of love for the other person. If they have faith enough to realize that such actions are mortal sins and that to lead another into mortal sin is to harm him very seriously, they can be encouraged to let their very love for the other, be it Christian charity or romantic love, provide the brakes.

The Church has always extolled virginity, and the Western Church has long required celibacy of her priests. It is very important that the Church's aim in these questions be well understood. One hears a lot of nonsense on the subject. It is sometimes said that this is another indication that the Church really takes a dim view of sex, when you come right down to it, and that her attitude is that marriage is all right for those who are too weak and imperfect to get along without sex, but the elite should be above anything so sordid. This, of course, is a caricature of the Church's view of sex and marriage. Another allegation is that a group of celibate priests can live together in a rectory easily, whereas three or four priests with wives and families would not be able to. This is a foolish argument. It might be a very good thing if priests lived throughout the parish rather than together in one house. They might have better contact with the people if they were decentralized in this fashion. At any rate, those priests of the Eastern Rites who are married seem to have no trouble about this; neither do the Orthodox and Anglican clergy.

The reason the Church extols virginity is a profound one. It is not that she thinks less of marriage but rather that she recognizes that there is something even better than marriage. Marriage is the usual way the individual finds fulfillment. One human being binds himself to another. He gives himself to another and receives from that other. He centers his love upon one person. It is through this binding and being bound in love, through this giving and receiving, that human love matures. It grows and extends, as we have said, to the family and to those outside the family. Nonetheless, it is centered on one person. St. Paul says:

> He who is unmarried is concerned about the things of the Lord, how he may please God. Whereas he who is married is concerned about the things of the world, how he may please his wife; and he is divided. And the unmarried woman, and the virgin, thinks about the things of the Lord, that she may be holy in body and in spirit. Whereas she who is married thinks about the things of the world, how she may please her husband. [1 Cor 7:32–34]

These words of the apostle could easily be misunderstood. St. Paul is not saying that unmarried people are thereby spiritual and God-centered and that married people, by the very fact of being married, are worldly and self-centered. Experience, for one thing, would contradict this notion. Christian marriage leads people to closer intimacy with God, and by its very nature has the effect of making people unselfish. Everyone has seen the self-centered, crusty old bachelor and the finicky, selfish "old maid," both of whom compare very unfavorably with the unselfish, generous-hearted married people who are all about us. Moreover, every priest and religious can testify that he meets married people whose holiness is such as to put him to shame.

What St. Paul is saying is that *ideally* consecrated virginity provides a means of freeing the whole person so that he can devote himself entirely to the love of God and of all men. It is a question of much more than time, although usually an unmarried person has more time to devote to prayer and works of charity. It is a question of the freeing of one's whole self, all one's physical and psychic energies, all one's gifts of manliness or womanliness. Undeniably, a married person has the duty of using these energies primarily for the good of his family. The energies of the celibate can have as their immediate object God Himself and all mankind, because no other human being has a claim on his heart.

Marriage and the sexual union have the effect of involving one person so deeply with another that this involvement is described as a merger of two in one flesh. The married person must give to his partner *and he must also receive*; were he to refuse to receive he would be false to his marriage vows, to his pledge, "I *take* thee," by which he has opened himself to another and received the gift of another person. The person who has a vow of chastity has vowed himself totally to God and to the children of God. When he gives himself to others, as he must by his very vow of chastity, it is without the involvement which necessarily comes with sexual union. He must give himself to others *without receiving in return*. His is a lifelong gift of self not to one person but to whoever needs him.

This is the ideal which the Church holds up. It is hardly necessary to point out that it is not always attained.

Those who have a vow of chastity always run the risk of using their freedom to enjoy their own leisure rather than to give themselves to others. Without the demands of marriage and family life, which usually cause a person to become outgoing and unselfish, there is always the danger that one may simply become self-centered and set in one's ways. This can be true of a person who is consecrated by a vow as it can be of the lay person who, for one reason or another, remains unmarried. In both cases chastity must be practiced. The person must go out of his narrow self and put himself and his energies at the service of God and of his fellow men. The words of St. Paul do not apply to the person who remains unmarried in order to be able to live in his own selfish way, free from the commitments and responsibilities of married life. They do not apply either to the person with a vow who does not give his undivided heart to God and his neighbor. If the priest who stated that he sat in his chair all day simply practicing celibacy really did just that, he was a failure. Celibacy did not do for him what the Church meant it to do. It turned him into a selfish bachelor rather than a spiritual father.

If, on the other hand, any Christian, whatever his state of life, cultivates chastity as it is to be lived within his state of life, he will be more fully a person because he does so and much more closely fashioned in the image of Christ, the perfect man and the perfect model of chastity.

9

Charity Never Fails

Many of us, unfortunately, do not examine our consciences the way the Lord will examine them for us on the Last Day. We say, "Let me see—did I lie? Did I swear? Did I have bad thoughts?" The Lord will say something rather different: "Did you feed me when I was hungry? Did you clothe me? Did you see that I found shelter when I had no place to live? Did you visit me when I was in prison?" At least, this is what our Lord Himself tells us—that at the Last Judgment He will say:

> Come, blessed of my Father, take possession of the kingdom prepared for you from the foundation of the world; for I was hungry and you gave me to eat; I was thirsty and you gave me to drink; I was a stranger and you took me in; naked and you covered me; sick and you visited me; I was in prison and you came to me. . . . Amen I say to you, as long as you did it for one of these, the least of my brethren, you did it for me. [Mt 25:34–36, 40]

Our Lord speaks as though what we have come to call the corporal works of mercy will be the only criterion by which we will be judged; He says nothing about how many rosaries we might have said or how many novenas we might have made, nothing even about the commandments of God or the laws of the Church. Does this mean that we should give up the rosary and forget about the commandments? Obviously not. What it does mean, though, is that saying prayers and keeping laws are not enough; we must love everyone, see Christ in everyone, and actually treat every person as we would treat Christ Himself.

The seventh commandment tells us that we must not steal from our fellow man; more positively, it tells us that we must give every man what is his due. And Our Lord tells us that we must go farther and give every man not only what is his due but whatever he needs in order to live a truly human life. Actually, this considerably simplifies the whole business of what is to be given to others.

What is due to a man in justice? To what does he have a strict right? In today's extremely complex economic and social order, this is not always easy to determine. Not too many years ago even Catholic businessmen would have said that a worker was entitled only to whatever he agreed to work for. Popes Leo XIII and Pius XI condemned this idea as unjust, and stated that a just wage is one which is sufficient to enable a man and his family to live decently and with security. Centuries ago, in a very simple economy, it was easy to fix a price on an article and regard it as a just price. Nowadays, a raising of prices in a basic industry such as steel can have a devastating effect on the whole economy. There are complicated issues like featherbedding which become all the more serious as automation grows. Surely the teaching on justice which served very well in the thirteenth century is no longer adequate.

The popes of modern times have been faithful to their teaching office. In their encyclicals they have applied the principles of Christian morality to modern social and economic questions. It is here, in these encyclicals, that the teaching of the Church is to be found, not in a catechism which defines the virtue of justice in only the broadest terms. All intelligent Catholics ought to be familiar with the encyclicals, which show how not only the seventh commandment but also the corporal works of mercy are to be practiced today.

The popes make a distinction between justice and charity, as do the experts. This is an important theological point. But while there are cases in which it makes a difference on the practical level for the ordinary Catholic, is not the Christian life based on charity anyway? In practice a lot of perfectly valid but difficult distinctions are swept away by the simple fact that here and now I give this man what he needs, whether I owe it to him in justice or simply because he is Christ and is in need. In theory, a pastor is bound in justice to go out on a sick call to give the sacraments to a dying parishioner. His assistant is bound in charity, not in justice, to do so. But what a strange situation it would be if the younger priest were to insist that the older priest take the call since he has the stricter obligation! In theory, it might be argued that I could sell a car which needs a serious motor overhaul, saying nothing about it, on the assumption that the buyer should know that any five-year-old car would require such an overhaul. In practice, would not a Christian instinctively realize that the thing to do would be to have the job done first or at least tell the buyer the real condition of the car? Shakespeare put it very well when he said that mercy must season justice. Our Lord put it better when He said that we must treat others as we would treat Him.

There are few terms more unfortunate than the expression "corporal works of mercy." The words make the whole business seem remote and unreal—*works* which are to be *performed* for the *bodies of others*. There they are, on the page of a catechism. They seem to stand out in isolation, off in the air somewhere. They sound like terms which came from the pen of a theologian rather than words which came from the lips of Christ—"I was hungry and you gave me to eat." But there is another problem, too. Even when we come to realize that these "works of mercy" come to us from the lips of Christ and are the essential expression of Christian love, they seem strangely unreal and impractical today. How can you feed the hungry when everyone you know has enough to eat? How can you go and visit prisoners when they won't let anyone but relatives of the inmates inside the prison? How can you be expected to welcome into your home a stranger who might well run off with the silverware or even cut your throat?

One good Catholic housewife did try to put the injunction to do works of mercy into application, as far as she thought it compatible with prudence. She was shown up by her five-year-old son, who had a more literal and direct approach. The good lady opened the door one morning and found a ragged stranger standing there. He asked for something to eat. As the man ate the breakfast the housewife gave him, he told her his story. He was a migrant worker who had left his family behind and come to this place, seeking work in the fields. He worked hard picking berries all day and, having no place to go at night, slept in the open fields. The housewife remembered the words of Christ. She offered to let the man sleep in her basement, which could be locked off from the rest of the house. "Here," she thought, "is a chance to explain to Tommy what Christian charity means." She told her five-year-old about the man and explained that she was treating him this way because he was Christ. Little Tommy took it all in very seriously and then asked, "But Mommie, why is Christ living in the *basement?*"

The housewife, of course, had a valid motive for her action: it would not be prudent to give a stranger the run of one's house. How, then, is one to practice the corporal works of mercy?

Nowadays, we are apt to reflect that we still perform the corporal works of mercy, but in an indirect way. By donating to the collection for the Catholic charities every year, we help provide food and shelter for those in need. The annual clothing drive provides an opportunity not only to clean out the closets but also to clothe the naked wherever they might be. Yet some Christians find themselves uneasy every now and then when they stop to think about it. The trouble is that while such contributions are charity, they are utterly impersonal. There is a great deal of difference between giving money in a collection and taking the trouble to help the needy directly. In the one case you give money; in the other you give yourself directly. A priest who is called down to the office to find a woman in a ragged housedress with a tale of financial woe faces this problem very often. It is far easier to give her a dollar or two and let it go at that than to call at the home, check on the story, size up the whole situation, and go about getting the help which the family needs. It is a question of becoming involved with people. This is what is hard; this takes time and trouble.

Yet it is difficult to imagine that Jesus was speaking of impersonal contributions to drives and collections when He said, "I was hungry and you gave me to eat." The "I" refers to a personal relationship, to a person-to-person encounter. This is not to say, of course, that we should not contribute, and generously, to such causes; we have a definite duty in charity to do so. But the real practice of the corporal works of mercy does not end there.

There is still the question of practicality, however. How does one do these things in the circumstances of modern life? First of all, we should realize that when Christ said, "I was hungry and you gave me to eat," and "I was thirsty and you gave me to drink," He was speaking in the colorful, concrete Oriental manner which was natural and familiar to Him and to His listeners. These works of mercy are examples rather than theological formulae. What Christ was really saying was, "I was in need and you came to my assistance." If it is a corporal work of mercy to give a drink to a thirsty man, why it is not also a corporal work of mercy to give a cigarette to someone who is "dying for a smoke?" If it is a corporal work of mercy to visit the sick, why is it not also a corporal work of mercy to donate a television set to a lonely old lady? The catechism says that there are seven corporal works of mercy. It is hardly conceivable that Jesus was preoccupied with the number. Terminology is not what counts, but serving Christ in others and helping them, whatever their need.

A couple moved into a new apartment. They knew no one in the neighborhood. The apartment was a mess. It was during wartime, when you were lucky to find an apartment at all and had to do your own cleaning and decorating. The second night there was a knock on the kitchen door. There stood the couple who lived upstairs. They were fully armed with a stepladder, buckets, cloths, and brushes. "Hi," they announced. "We thought you could use some help in getting the place fixed up." This couple was not concerned with terminology; they simply saw that someone else needed help and they were willing to give that help, even to the extent of becoming personally involved. It so happened that the new tenant was a fallen-away Catholic and his wife had no religion. The man came back to the Church and the wife became a Catholic. Both later stated that the first step in their conversion was the example of the Catholic couple upstairs who had knocked on their kitchen door that night. But all this had nothing to do with the decision of the couple upstairs to help; they knew nothing about the people downstairs except that they needed help. That was all they needed to know.

A pastor of a large urban parish once received a bitter letter which bore a name and address. It was from a woman who described herself as a "former Catholic and a former parishioner." She stated in the letter that she had given up in disgust. She and her husband had agreed that Catholics were fakers. They talked about loving their neighbors but did nothing about it. The pastor called at the house. He found a young housewife with four little children. The woman was on the point of exhaustion. The couple had lived there for almost a year and yet were not well acquainted with any of the neighbors. They could not afford to pay a baby-sitter, and had not had an evening out in years. The pastor called together several married couples in the parish. They discussed the matter and developed a plan.

They called on the couple who were in distress and arranged a free baby-sitting service. They spoke to the neighbors, some of whom proved to be more than willing to be friendly. They just had been unaware that this couple had been in any need at all.

A Christian who is sensitive to the needs of others sees without having to be told that all about him there are people who need his love and attention. There are couples who allow and encourage their teen-age daughters to baby-sit only where they will not be paid. These people are able to apply the works of mercy to the modern scene. Our Lord might well have said, "I needed a few hours of recreation and you baby-sat for me."

Actually, it is a mistake to think that the "original" corporal works of mercy are impractical in modern life, even the idea of welcoming a stranger into one's home. Many American families make it possible for young people of other countries to come to the United States for an education by welcoming them into their homes as one of the family during the time of their schooling. One married man who was attending a special course at a university noticed two men from India in one of his classes. He went up to them, introduced himself to them, and invited them to his home for Sunday dinner. The two accepted eagerly. Later they explained that although they were teachers, educated and cultured men, they had been treated very coldly during their stay in the United States. One of them told him, "You are the first American who is not a Communist to invite us into your home. I was about to leave your country with bitterness in my heart against Americans. Because of you I feel different." This act of kindness had a good effect as far as foreign relations are concerned. But that is not the point. Nor was it the motive of the man who performed the act of mercy. He wanted simply to show love and hospitality to strangers.

Even the seemingly impossible undertaking of visiting those who are in prison can be done. A certain Catholic couple can arrange such a visit for anyone who wishes to cooperate with them in a great work of Christian charity which they have undertaken. It started when it was brought to this couple's attention that the reasons most ex-convicts wound up back in prison was that they could not find a job on the outside. Being rebuffed again and again, they became discouraged and returned to crime as a means of livelihood. In cases where a prisoner had a job waiting for him as soon as he was released, they learned, the chances of his keeping on the straight and narrow were very good. Another couple might have simply expressed the hope that something could be done about the situation, and let the matter drop there. Not this couple—and they were not, be it noted, childless with time on their hands. They had two children of their own, four adopted children, and a teen-age foreign student living in their home. They decided to do something about finding jobs for men who were about to be released from prison. They got the cooperation of chaplains and wardens, and enlisted the aid of other men and women to help in interviewing the prisoners, giving them examinations to determine their capabilities. They talked to employers, explaining the problem and asking them to give these men a chance. The result has been a wonderful work of rehabilitation which continues to go on year after year.

One of the marks of a mature Christian is that he sees

the oneness of humanity. He sees the human race as God sees it—as one family. The popes have continually pointed out that human life in all its ramifications must be built on cooperation among men; there must be mutual aid and assistance, and those who have more must help those that have less. The works of mercy apply to nations as well as to individuals. It is astonishing that people who would never think of sitting idly by and refusing to help relatives or even next-door neighbors who do not have enough to eat object strenuously to our government's giving aid to nations whose people are undernourished and in want. It is even more astonishing to hear the remark from Christians, "These people don't appreciate what you do for them anyway"—as if that had anything to do with it.

Jesus did not say that we were to show mercy only to those who would appreciate it. He Himself acted otherwise. He knew perfectly well that nine of the ten lepers He cured would not return to thank Him. Our Lord even went so far as to help those who He knew would hurt Him in return. When Jesus saw a wretched old paralytic lying alongside the pool of Bethsaida, His only reaction was pity. He cured the man without waiting to be asked. "Rise, take up thy pallet and walk," Jesus told him. Some Pharisees, seeing the man rolling up his pallet, said to him, "It is the Sabbath; thou art not allowed to take up thy pallet." The man replied, "He who made me well said to me, 'Take up thy pallet and walk.'" The Pharisees demanded to know the name of the one who had not only worked a cure on the Sabbath but also ordered another to do what they considered a violation of the Lord's Day. The man replied that he did not know who it was that had cured him. He would have told them had he known. Evidently this miserable little man was anxious to curry favor with the authorities, because as soon as he discovered who it was he ran as fast as his restored legs could carry him and reported Jesus to His enemies, giving them more ammunition against Him. Yet Jesus had deliberately sought him out in the temple in order to help him again, this time with the warning, "Sin no more, lest something worse befall thee" (Jn 5:8–14).

It is a strange thing indeed to find people with no religion agreeing that the wealthiest nation in the world should give assistance to poor and underdeveloped countries while some Christians object on the grounds that it increases their taxes and that the recipients will still not refuse to speak to the Russians. One would think that Christians would rejoice that their country, for whatever reasons, practices works of mercy. Those whose motives are purely political would be disappointed if no political good resulted. A Christian should be satisfied that the hungry are being fed and the homeless housed, and let it go at that.

We cannot say that the world is so organized today that the corporal works of mercy are no longer practical. It may take an organization to find shelter for the homeless—like those which seek out decent housing for Negroes who are paying three times as much rent for a rat-infested flat in a slum as white people do in a fine neighborhood. Very well, what is to prevent a Christian from assisting this organization? It would seem to be undeniable that any efforts to root out the terrible housing conditions which segregation causes come under the heading of a corporal work of mercy —even talking, even writing letters to the newspapers or to aldermen or congressmen.

The fact remains, moreover, that on every level, including the personal, these basic manifestations of Christian love are practical and necessary. As long as there are people, this will be so. There will always be those around us who are in need. But even to see them it is necessary to ask the right question—not "What is due to him?" but "What does he need?"

There is a connection between the works of mercy and something which every now and then gnaws a bit at the consciences of Christians—the idea of Christian poverty. It is impossible to read the Gospels without being struck by the way Christ spoke of poverty and the example He gave regarding the poor. When a Scribe, in a burst of generosity, offered to follow Jesus wherever He went, our Lord said, "The foxes have dens, the birds of the air have nests, but the Son of Man has nowhere to lay His head." When a rich young man came to Him, seeking the way to perfection, Jesus told him, "If thou wilt be perfect, go, sell what thou hast and give to the poor, and thou shalt have treasure in heaven." Then, as the young man walked sadly away, our Lord spoke those strange and frightening words: "With what difficulty will they who have riches enter the kingdom of God! For it is easier for a camel to pass through an eye of a needle, than for a rich man to enter the kingdom of God." And when Christ gave the picture of what a Christian should be, He began with the words, "Blessed are the poor in spirit, for theirs is the kingdom of heaven."

How is a Christian who is living in the world to practice poverty? Is a family with a comfortable home supposed to sell it and move into the slums? Hardly. One of the objectives of the Church is to improve the financial conditions of all people; we would all like to do away with slums, and for that matter, with poverty. What meaning, then, has poverty in the life of a Christian who lives in an affluent society? Does it mean giving up luxuries? What would happen to the economy of the country if everyone used his automobile until it fell apart and kept his television set, radio, and electric shaver until they were beyond repair? Workers who are now living in moderate comfort would be on breadlines. And what, after all, is a luxury? Two automobiles might well be a necessity for suburban families. An actress or the wife of the President needs a different type of wardrobe from that of the ordinary housewife. One social worker remarked that she hardly ever finds a family without a television set, no matter how poor they are. Contrary to orders, she never reports the fact that they have one or tells them that they must sell it; she regards the television set as a necessity for these poor people.

Perhaps the norm of Christian poverty is to be found not in how much a man has but in how he uses what he has. In Christ's parable of Lazarus and the rich man, the rich man went to hell not because he was rich but because he refused to help Lazarus. Here is the connection between the works of mercy and poverty. Will not the Christian be practicing poverty by using what he has for the cause of God and the good of his neighbor? Simply being apostolic and charitable necessitates detachment and generosity, and calls for sacrifices which are really part of the practice of poverty. The couple who take foreign students into their home are not thinking in terms of poverty. Yet they are practicing it to the extent that they are incurring an expense for the sake of charity. The couple who pay for a babysitter in order to attend meetings of an organization of the lay apostolate are practicing poverty in this sense also. One young man gave up a good job to attend the Institute of Lay Theology and train himself to work as a lay instructor of converts in a parish. He thought of his action only in terms of the apostolate, but it was certainly a matter of poverty and detachment, too. The same is true of those who go to the missions as lay missionaries for a year or more and those who spend their vacations helping out in missionary parishes in the South and Southwest.

Many Catholics contribute regularly to an astonishingly large number of missionary and charitable organizations without thinking of their generosity in terms of poverty. Yet they could use this money for luxuries for themselves. Parents make great sacrifices to give their children a good Catholic education. This, too, is the practice of poverty.

The poor in spirit in the Old Testament were people who strove to do the will of God no matter what suffering was entailed. They were despised and persecuted by the wealthy and powerful. Their love of God and their neighbor cost them a great deal. These are the people of whom Christ spoke in the beatitudes. The Christian is to be poor in spirit in this sense. His love of God and devotion to principle will cost him something. The man whose store is boycotted by the White Citizens' Council because his conscience moved him to sign a manifesto on the rights of Negroes is poor in spirit. The teacher who does not get an increase in salary because he spoke up for academic freedom, the man who is not promoted because he objected to unethical business practices—these, too, are poor in spirit. In our materialistic and acquisitive society, the person who tries to advance the Kingdom of God will very often pay for his convictions in a monetary way.

The man who helps another in need without expecting payment is to some extent poor in spirit. Such a man is the lawyer who gives free legal advice to people who can't afford to pay for it, or the doctor who charges people who are very poor little or nothing and who works in clinics and hospitals in the slums.

The more one grows in the love of Christ, the more one sees and feels the needs of others and the more one makes sacrifices for others. The needs of others become so real that luxuries are renounced and economy practiced for the sake of charity. A man buys a less expensive suit and gives the amount saved to someone in need. One woman sold a beautiful diamond ring and gave the money to an apostolic group which was in financial trouble, explaining that she did not feel right wearing the ring when God's work needed help.

The mere renunciation of wealth is not what Christ had in mind when He spoke to the rich young man. Jesus told him to give his wealth to the poor and to come and follow Him. Christian maturity involves not that frugality which is part of Puritanism but that poverty of spirit which is part of mercy, charity, and the apostolic spirit.

10

The Layman and the Church Today

A priest who worked for many years as a missionary in Japan described the procedure he used in instructing converts. In his first instruction he would explain why he, a European, had taken the trouble to learn the Japanese language and Japanese customs, why he had left his own country and come halfway across the world to live among strangers. "It is because I am a Christian," he would tell the people. "A Christian is one who loves Christ, and therefore he wants others to know and love Christ also." At the very next class the missionary would startle his catechumens by demanding to know why they had returned alone. He would appear to be shocked that each person had not brought at least one friend or relative along to the class. "If you are going to be a Christian," he would tell them, "you must be as an apostle of Jesus Christ. You must never keep to yourself what you have come to know about Christ. You must tell others about Him. You must bring others to this class so that they may come to know and love Him, too."

This procedure usually strikes "cradle Catholics" back home as a very good and sensible one—for catechumens in

Japan. Many would think it out of place, however, in Philadelphia or Boston or Denver. Back home, where religion is well established, respectability requires, some think, a quiet, unobtrusive practice of the faith and a decent reticence in speaking about it, especially to outsiders. The reason for this attitude is often a quite laudable desire not to be a religious freak or fanatic. It is sometimes a reaction to the zealots of certain sects who, many feel, do more harm than good to the cause of religion. But is it always merely this? Isn't it sometimes a sign of a diluted, compromised kind of Christianity, a Christianity which concentrates on personal piety and excludes that apostolic zeal which is an essential of Christianity? In a word, is this personalized, inbred form of Christianity another example of religious immaturity?

The mature Christian sees life as it is. The mature Catholic sees the Church as it is and realizes the part he has to play in the life and worship of the Church; his prayer life is not the individualistic piety which finds expression in purely personal, often sentimental and theologically off-center devotions. He understands the meaning of the Mass and the sacraments and knows their full familial nature. He sees faith as a full commitment of his entire person to God, as something to be lived and not merely accepted by the intellect or professed by the tongue. He sees Christian morality as love of God and of neighbor expressed in living. But even all this, important as it is, would not be enough. To be a mature Catholic, a man must see the Church as Christ. He must understand her true nature and know her mission, which is not only to save souls but also to help bring men and the world in which men live to full perfection. Only if he has this understanding and knowledge will the Catholic be able to take part in the work of the Church, the work of Christ, as a mature Catholic.

There are those who see the Church as a sort of supernatural insurance company that guarantees Heaven to those who keep the laws and use their Sunday envelopes regularly. The Church, for them, exists only to get them to Heaven—to get *them*, not necessarily other people. The Church, they believe, has nothing to do with the world. An example of this type of Catholic is the man who bristles when he hears a sermon on social matters. "Why should we hear sermons on stuff like housing and segregation?" he complains. What he wants is a nice little homily which avoids bringing the teachings of Christ into contact with the modern world. He is convinced that the Church has no business getting involved with the problems of this life—let her stick to "pie in the sky when we die."

There are those who fail to see the mystery of the Church. For them it is all very simple. We are the good guys; we are going to Heaven; we know all the answers. They think that those outside the Church are stupid not to see that the Catholic Church is the one true Church of Jesus Christ. He founded it; He said, "On this rock I will build my church"; He made the Pope infallible. These people also take great pride in the material accomplishments of the Church—the buildings and institutions, the prosperity of the Church, the victories of Catholic college football teams. They are genuinely and unquestioningly loyal to the Church and churchmen. They know well the juridical aspects of the Church, and know nothing of her inner life. They see the Church as a vast organization founded by Christ and watched over from the outside, as it were, by the Holy Spirit. They do not see her as the Mystical Christ, as the very Body of Christ, as Christ Himself. They do not realize that just as Christ has two aspects, the visible human aspect which is His human nature and the invisible, divine aspect of His divinity, so the Church has both a visible, juridical structure and an inner life, the life of Christ which we share as we live in union with Christ and with one another, vivified and united by the Soul of the Church, the Holy Spirit. Catholics who do not see the inner life of the Church fail to realize that they are part of that life and therefore part of the Church. They think they are meant to take orders and be taught. They do not grasp the mission of the Church or see their part in it.

There are Catholics, too, who see the Church merely as a huge bureau to which they can come for service. It is something which fulfills their spiritual needs. They can go to it to "get" the sacraments and the sacramentals, to express themselves in their prayers and devotions, and to receive advice and consolation. These people also love the Church, but they love her as if she were in some sense their private possession. They think of the Church as something which exists in order to serve them. They are quite willing to serve the Church in return, to support it financially and to work in the ham and bacon booth at the parish carnival, but they do not see the real Church. These Catholics, too, fail to see the mission of the Church, and lacking this vision, they are unable to take part as mature Catholics in the Church's work.

The mature Catholic sees, above all, that the Church is a profound mystery. It is nothing so simple as a mere juridical organization which is divinely established and endowed with a promise of infallibility, or so parochial as a bureau of service. It is the mystery of Christ. It is the whole Christ. It is Christ, the Incarnate Word, incarnated into humanity, into the world. It is Christ transforming the world, Christ applying His redemption to everything in the world. It is Christ worshiping the Father and bringing all men to the Father. It is Christ in us and we in Christ.

Imperfect indeed is the concept of the Church as a religious organization which exists merely to save the souls of individuals. The Church is not *of* the world but she is very much *in* the world, and she is very much interested in the world. This world was made by God; it was redeemed by Christ. God put man into the world as the lord of creation. He made man His steward over all the things He had created. It is through man that God continues to create; it is through man that God brings all things to a head in Christ. The mission of the Church is to establish the Kingdom of God in the whole world, and in so doing to develop that world and everything in it to its full perfection. It would be as serious a misunderstanding of the Church's mission, therefore, to see it as something which concerns only souls, not men, as it would be to think that the Church should be concerned only with men themselves and not also with the world in which they live.

If the Church must be interested in everything which concerns man, she must be interested in the economic order, which provides a human living for man; she must be interested in the social order, in housing and urban renewal, in civil rights, in education; she must be interested in world issues, in underdeveloped countries, in emerging nations, in international organizations, in problems of population.

The social encyclicals of popes of modern times bear witness to the Church's right and duty to be active in all these fields.

But the work of the Church in the world is not confined to the social and economic order; the Church must help mankind develop in every field of knowledge and culture. Therefore, she must be interested in art, in music, in architecture, in literature, in science—in everything which contributes to the discovery of truth. A seminarian was once asked by a man sitting next to him on a train what subjects he was studying in the seminary. The young man listed the subjects. Among them were music and art appreciation. The questioner grunted. "Why do you have to know things like that to be a priest?" he asked. He did not understand that a priest is a man, and that to be a fully developed man he has to develop all his faculties and capabilities.

The Church is interested in helping all men become fully human; therefore, she is interested in the education of the whole man. Pope Pius XII gave evidence of this by speaking and writing on an unbelievably large number of subjects, and untiringly encouraging study and development in every field. It was fitting that the ship which carried Columbus on his great voyage of exploration was named the Santa Maria; it is equally fitting that the Church has special blessings for automobiles and for space rockets. These, too, are part of God's world; therefore, they are involved in the mission of the Church.

This mission of the Church, this work of the Church, is the work of the whole Church, a truth which is directly inferred from the irrefutable fact that the Church is a body, a living organism. Every part of a living organism has its function within that organism, and that function is always related to the good of the whole organism. If the Church were all bishops and priests it would not be the Church, any more than it would be if she were all laymen. The diversity of function within the Church was beautifully described by St. Paul when he wrote to the Christians at Corinth:

> For the body is not one member, but many. If the foot says, "Because I am not a hand, I am not of the body," it is therefore not of the body? And if the ear says, "Because I am not an eye, I am not of the body," is it therefore not of the body?
>
> If the whole body were an eye, where would be the hearing? If the whole body were hearing, where would be the smelling? But as it is, God has set the members, each of them, in the body as he willed. Now if they were all one member, where would the body be? But as it is, there are indeed many members, yet but one body. And the eye cannot say to the hand, "I do not need thy help"; nor again the head to the feet, "I have no need of you." . . .
>
> Now you are the body of Christ, member for member. And God indeed has placed some in the Church, first apostles, secondly prophets, thirdly teachers. . . . Are all apostles? Are all teachers? [1 Cor 12:14–21, 27–29]

Is not the Catholic whose attitude is, "I am not supposed to do anything apostolic; after all, I'm not a priest," really saying, "Because I am not a hand, I am not of the body"? His immaturity is showing. He does not fully grasp the idea of the Church, and does not understand his own vocation as a Catholic layman.

For the sake of sheer efficiency, but even more important, for the better apostolic development of all concerned, some straightening out is needed on the question of functions within the Church. Layman will better understand what their proper work is when it is left to them to do it; some confusion is caused by the fact that people are doing other people's jobs. Many priests today are employed full time doing what a layman could and really should be doing. It is odd to talk about a shortage of priests in a diocese when priests are working full time on newspapers, in various diocesan agencies, and in schools teaching algebra and English. Sometimes the shoe is on the other foot. There is a Catholic undertaker who is in the habit of preaching a sermon at the graveside. Other undertakers refer to him as "the Bishop." One priest's housekeeper folded her hands, fixed the assistant with a fierce stare, and announced, "The pastor just left on a trip. He told me to tell you that I am in charge in his place." Later, when a sick call came in, the assistant walked into the kitchen and handed the housekeeper the holy oils, stole, and ritual.

It is much more common, however, to find priests burdened with work which lay people would be perfectly willing and able to do. Why should a priest be a basketball coach? Why should he be doing secretarial work? Why, for that matter, should he be opening duplex envelopes and counting the Sunday collection? To say that priests are the only ones who can be trusted with the collection is not only foolish and untrue, it is downright libelous. And the argument that it is better to have a priest teaching English because he can be a good influence on the student is unflattering to Catholic laymen as well as unrealistic. Certainly, the influence of priests should be felt in a Catholic school, but it does not have to be felt in English class. One priest, who gives a marriage course to Catholic high-school boys, reports that the boys are much more impressed with the doctor and the young married couple he brings in at the end of the course than they are with him. They accept what he has to say about the Christian meaning of sex and the objections against birth control rather academically, as coming from a professional who is there to give them the official teaching. It is a different story when these Catholic young men hear a Catholic doctor speaking of the Christian concept of sex, and when they hear a couple who have to live day by day with the problems of married life talk about how a Christian faces up to issues like birth control.

This is not the important point, though. Surely, laymen should not be called in only to do jobs which will free priests. The layman has a role to play in assisting the priest in many things which are part of the Church's apostolate. But (and this is the heart of the matter) he also has specific functions to perform in the Church's apostolate which are his because he is a layman, functions which only he can perform effectively, functions which will not be performed at all unless Catholic laymen perform them.

First of all, regarding the layman's role as a helper to the priest, there are many fields in the apostolate in which laymen are needed. It would be fine if priests could call on every person in the parish personally and get to know the spiritual status, problems, and needs of his whole congregation. In practice, this is impossible except in very small parishes. Laymen are needed to help in census work, in making contact with fallen-away Catholics and couples with invalid marriages, and in uncovering many problems which the priest can then handle. In work of this sort, moreover, a layman can sometimes be particularly effective. One parish in an all-Negro neighborhood used volunteers from another parish to ring every doorbell in the neighborhood and invite the people to come to Mass. One woman, who not only accepted the invitation but also later became a Catholic, had this reaction: "I figured that if this white man left his warm house on a cold day to come and invite me to look into his religion, that religion must mean a lot to him." This lady took it for granted that a priest's religion would mean a lot to him. What impressed her especially was that her caller was a layman.

This same parish has provided many services for the people of the neighborhood by making use of laymen and laywomen. A charm school was begun, in which girls who had the advantage of training in taste taught the neighborhood girls how to dress attractively and in good taste as well as many other things which helped them to be at ease in social gatherings and to be eligible for better jobs. College students tutored boys and girls who had dropped out of high school and had found that their lack of education prevented them from getting a job.

Many pastors have discovered that they can have the kind of participation in the liturgy the Church wants them to have if they enlist the help of laymen. They train laymen to read the Scripture readings at liturgical services and to act as leaders of the congregation. The use of laymen in this capacity often proves to be a blessing for everyone. It gives the people a realization of the part the laity have to play in Church worship, and it provides a real spiritual experience for the men who take part. One man, who had been acting as leader of the congregation at Mass for about a year, wrote to his pastor at Christmas, "You will never know what effect this has had on my spiritual life."

Laymen have been working in such apostolic organizations as the Legion of Mary and the St. Vincent de Paul Society for so long that their participation is now regarded as traditional. Everyone recognizes the fact that the men and women in these organizations are doing an important work which is part of the Church's mission. Nowadays there is an increasing tendency to use lay people to teach religion. The Confraternity of Christian Doctrine trains them to teach religion to public school students and, in some places, to give part or all of the necessary instructions in the faith to prospective converts. Lay instructors in one parish give the instructions in the homes of the prospective converts.

Laymen who are active in work of this kind are really carrying on a practice which began in the earliest days of the Church. After the death of St. Stephen, the first Catholic martyr, a persecution broke out in Jerusalem, we read in the Acts of the Apostles. "Now those who had been dispersed by the persecution . . . ," Scripture tells us, "went all the way to Phoenicia and Cyprus and Antioch, speaking the word to none except to Jews only. But some of them were Cyprians and Cyreneans, who on reaching Antioch began to speak to the Greeks also, preaching the Lord Jesus. And the hand of the Lord was with them, and a great number believed and turned to the Lord" (Acts 11:19–21). Laymen in the early Church realized very well that they had a part to play in spreading the faith. They called in the apostles to give Confirmation, but they did not hesitate to seize every opportunity to spread the Gospel.

It is salutary for modern Catholics to consider the zeal of the Mormons, for example, whose young men give two or more years of their lives working full time as apostles. Modern Catholics are doing this, too. More and more lay people, single and married, are signing up and going to the missions for certain specified times and working as full-time missionaries. They are an immense help to the priests and sisters, and they make a special contribution simply because they are lay people. It is something like the doctor and the young married couple in the high-school marriage course; people see how Catholics live the Christian life, and come to understand that it is not something merely for priests and nuns. This must have been what was in mind of Pius XII when he said that nine lay people and one priest could be more effective in the missions than ten priests.

In addition to the layman's work in the Church as helper to the priest, he has a great work which is part of the Church's mission and which only he, not the hierarchy and not the priests, can do. This is the work of the Church in the world, the work of bringing the world and everything in it to its full development. Here is the field in which the Catholic layman is to do his specific work as a layman, the place where he belongs because of his vocation and where he must do the Church's work if that work is to be done at all. The layman is the Church in the temporal order, in which men work and govern and engage in the business of living. The immature Catholic layman is of no use here—the man who believes that business is one thing and morality another, the man who thinks that work is something apart from his spiritual life, the man who rails against Communism but sees no connection between it and bad housing, racial discrimination, and poverty, the man who regards the world as hopeless and tries to escape from it and its demands. In the temporal order, the Church needs fully formed members who are conscious of their Christian vocation, who see the work to be done and are not afraid to tackle it.

The Church's mission in the temporal order includes two activities: the enunciation of the Christian principles which must govern both the individual man as he lives and works and the institutions which serve man and supply his needs, and the application of those principles to the concrete issues and problems of life. The first work is done by the teaching Church. This is the work of the hierarchy, the Pope and the bishops, in the papal encyclicals and episcopal statements and pastorals, and of the priests, who preach and teach the doctrine which the hierarchy sets forth. The application of these principles to concrete legislation, to concrete situations, to concrete issues is the work of the Catholic layman. Who but he can bring the teachings of the Church from the pages of an encyclical to the floor of the Senate or a board of directors' meeting or a union meeting or a bull session in the local tavern? Here is where the layman lives, works, takes his recreation.

The Church today finds herself in a situation different from anything she knew in the past. This is a phenomenon which has repeated itself at various times in the Church's history. Each time, she has adapted herself to the new situation and gone about her work of establishing the Kingdom of God in the world in whose midst she found herself. When the Church moved into the great world of Greco-Roman civilization, she adapted herself to that world and set about to establish in it the Kingdom of God. When she found herself amid the ruins of the Roman Empire and confronted with barbarians, she adapted herself once again and gave herself to the immense task of converting these peoples and guiding them in building a new civilization.

Today, the Church finds herself in the midst of a new world, one which is urban and highly industrialized. Once again, she is in the process of adapting herself. The influence of the Holy Spirit in bringing about this adaptation is to be seen in many ways. It is most evident in the almost unbelievable achievements of Pope John XXIII during his short reign, the work which he so aptly titled *aggiornamento,* bringing the Church up to date in the modern world. The Church today must face the problems of a world in the process of revolution, a world challenged by Communism and desperately in need of peace, justice, and brotherhood among men and nations if it is to survive at all, a world which has arrived at an unprecedented peak of scientific development but which has yet to learn how properly to use the knowledge and technical skill it has acquired.

In this world of the mid-twentieth century the Church needs an enlightened and fully mature laity as she has never needed them before. Laymen must be able and willing to work with their neighbors on matters which concern the community. They must realize that although their children are in Catholic schools, they have an obligation to see that the best kind of education is given to the children in the public schools. They must make it their task to work with others in the community to provide good housing for everybody, and be active in their labor unions or business associations, seeking to promote the common good. The mature layman is concerned with the welfare of men the world over, and willing and ready to promote organizations which seek to bring about peace, harmony and justice among men and nations. He knows that he is a Catholic doing the work of the Church in everything he does.

One Catholic layman, an executive in a telephone company, showed that he understood his role in the Church's mission. He put the Church's teaching on race into practice by seeing to it that Negroes were able to get good jobs in his company. Another puts Christian principles to work in the human relations committee with which he works. Catholic writers and artists and professional men have plenty of opportunities of doing this work in their fields, as do Catholic workers in their unions.

All Catholics have the opportunity of spreading the Church's teachings on race, on international relations, on all the burning issues of modern life. But the legalistic Catholic is of no use here. Neither is the Catholic who is out for "the best of two worlds," or the narrowly pietistic Catholic, or the one whose sole ambition is to "save his own soul" and who thinks he can do it by living in an ivory tower.

A Catholic young man who had been keeping steady company with a girl for eight months was asked what her religion was. He replied, "I have no idea. That is her own private affair." This is admittedly an extreme case, but it exemplifies an attitude which is not too uncommon. It should be apparent from the way a person acts that he believes certain things and has certain principles. If he has Christian principles they should show. Not, Heaven knows, that we should allow fanaticism to flourish. We should certainly not encourage the kind of person who "gets religion" and goes out to hit people over the head with it, like the woman who, after hearing a sermon, decided to go out and practice Catholic Action on her friends. She soon discovered that she no longer had any friends.

Living one's faith in the temporal order does not mean going about handing out pamphlets or Sacred Heart badges; it means doing one's job as a Christian. A good Catholic butcher would not give his customers a spiritual talk but would try to be the best kind of butcher he knows how to be, conscientious about his work and taking pride in his skill and efficiency, seeing and serving Christ in his customers. A good Catholic salesman does not sell religion but is honest and upright, strives to imitate Christ in his daily work, and does his part to put Catholic principles into practice by not padding expense accounts or engaging in shabby business practices. One Catholic salesman earned the respect and loyalty of his customers by being honest and considerate of them, even against the orders of his company. The company told their salesmen not to mention a forthcoming rise in price lest buyers stock up on material at the lower price. The salesman thought that such a practice would be unfair to his customers, and told them of the price rise.

A great work of the apostolate is that of giving good example. It is often said that the Church caused slavery to disappear in ancient Rome not by preaching but simply because individual Christians practiced charity and freed their slaves. Here is a case in which a revolution quietly occurred in the social order because of the individual actions of Catholic lay people. Could not a similar revolution be brought about in the case of modern issues which involve justice and charity?

First of all, however, Catholics must have the maturity to realize that the Church is deeply involved with the temporal order, that they are the Church in the temporal order, and that there is a job to be done. The first step in the formation of the lay apostolate is to open people's eyes to the world about them. There is an enormous change in the attitude of people at meetings of the Christian Family Movement after the first six months of attendance. At first they are honestly puzzled. There seem to be no problems, no social evils which need to be worked on, no opportunities to inject Christian attitudes. After six months or so of reading and discussing the Gospels and applying them to their own lives, of seeing the teachings of Christ and the Church in relation to the situations they do find, people discover evils they did not know existed and find problems of which they had been completely unaware. The world has not changed in these months; the people have. They have become Catholic in outlook. They have matured to the point where they can see the place of the Church in the temporal order. They have become aware of what the Church needs to do and of the fact that they are the Church doing it.

The immature Catholic is apt to see only what are called the religious problems which confront the Church, problems like leakage from the Church or divorce and birth control insofar as these things affect the Church. The mature Catholic sees that everything which concerns man, everything in which human society is involved, should be the concern of the Catholic layman. With this breadth of vision, he will find opportunities for positive and constructive action on all sides.

One Catholic layman who moved into a suburban town is a good case in point. He discovered that politics in the town was in a rut. There was only one political party. The same candidates ran again and again without opposition. There was no great trouble, no gross inefficiency, no scandalous dishonesty, but there was stagnation. The people displayed a spirit of indifference which made for an unproductive community life. The man went to work and formed an opposition party, believing that a one-party system was unhealthy. His party was alive and imaginative. It succeeded in taking over, with a vigorous, wide-awake administration. The new party was, in fact, so successful that the old party folded up. Thereupon this Catholic layman, consistent in his belief in the necessity of the two-party system, tried to persuade others to form another party in opposition to his own.

Pope John XXIII's great encyclical *Peace on Earth* caused a great stir throughout the world. It evoked editorials in secular newspapers and magazines in many countries. The letter was addressed not only to bishops, not only to priests, not only to Catholics even, but to all men of good will. It would be interesting to know how many Catholic lay people read this encyclical. How many read the many books and publications on Scripture and theology which are so readily available today? For religious maturity it is necessary to be really well informed on both the problems and issues of the day and the faith itself and everything which concerns it.

In these days of renewal, when the Church is rediscovering herself and presenting herself to the world in a more positive and dynamic way, there is a really imperative need for Catholics to have an up-to-date knowledge of their faith. If the layman is the Church in the temporal order, he must be fully formed and well informed in order to be effective. Much of his intellectual formation will come only from his own reading and study. His spiritual formation is his lifelong work, or rather the work of the Holy Spirit acting in him. The apostles were formed by the Holy Spirit in a moment on Pentecost. The lay apostle today is formed slowly, day by day, as he encounters Christ in the sacraments, communes with God in prayer, worships with his fellow members of Christ, and lives and works with others in daily life. Slowly, almost imperceptibly, the apostle is formed as he goes about doing his work of spreading the Kingdom of God. As he is led by the Spirit to a greater and greater resemblance to Christ, he grows to his full development as a man and as a Christian.